HIGHLI
ENGLISH
1

Susan Duberley

Heinemann Educational Publishers,
Halley Court, Jordan Hill, Oxford OX2 8EJ
a division of Reed Educational & Professional Publishing Ltd.

© Susan Duberley 1992

The moral rights of the author have been asserted.

First published 1992
96 97 11 10 9 8 7 6

British Library Cataloguing in Publication Data for this title is available from the British Library.

ISBN 0 435 10312 1

Designed by Ian Foulis

Cover photograph from Joy Myrdel

Printed and bound in Hong Kong

Acknowledgements
The author and publishers would like to thank the following for permission to reproduce copyright material:

The *Birmingham Post* for 'No Crisis of Identity as Boy Races to Pet; British Rail for British Rail tickets; Allan Cullen for extract from *John Willy and the Bee People*; Carcanet Press Ltd for 'The Computer's First Christmas Card' from *Collected Poems* by Edwin Morgan; Fast Forward for material on p30; Independent Television Publications Ltd for 'What I Watch' from TV Times; Look-In Magazine for extracts from Look-In on pp4 and 5; Methuen Children's Books for extract from *In the Net* by Michael Hardcastle; Metro Centre, Tyne & Wear for Metro Centre tickets; *The Observer* for 'Weather Traps' by Anne Vaughan; Gareth Owen for 'Half Asleep' and 'Winter' from *Song of the City*; Oxford University Press for extracts from *The Demon Headmaster* by Gillian Cross; Pan Macmillan Children's Books for extract from *Amaze and Amuse Your Friends* by Peter Eldin, Piccolo 1973; Penguin Books Ltd for 'Busy Day' by Michael Rosen from *You Tell Me* by Roger McGough and Michael Rosen, Kestrel Books, 1979; Random Century Group for extract from *Bad Boys* by Jim & Duncan Eldridge, Hutchinson 1987; Ian Serraillier for extract from *The Visitor* by Ian Serraillier; Tyne Valley Coaches Ltd for bus tickets; Russell, Vokening Inc for 'Yellow Butter' by Mary Ann Hoberman, © 1978; Ward Lock Educational for 'Irritating Sayings' from *Ways of Talking* by David Jackson; Hamish Whitely for *The Red Apple*.

We would also like to thank the following for permission to reproduce photographs on the pages noted:

J Allan Cash Ltd p5; Birmingham Post Ltd, p36 Channel 4 Television, p28; Rex Features/Sipa Press p4; Robert Harding Picture Library Ltd p32.

Contents

Unit 1: People and Places
Reading Preference chart   4
Comprehension; true or false   4
Making own preference charts   5
Listening to sound effects tape   6
Matching sounds in poem   6
Reading/comprehension of poem   6
Discussing poem   7
Describing/listening activity   7

Unit 2: Do's and Don'ts
Reading/comprehension of poem   8
Writing class poem   8
Discussion   9
Recording discussion   9
Sequencing paragraphs   10
Key words in paragraphs   11
Writing a letter   11

Unit 3: Word Games
Making a game (alphabet work)   12
Playing the game   12
Writing instructions for the game   12
Closer understanding of a poem   13
Compiling words ready for writing   13
Writing poem   13
Describing, remembering, listening   14
Understanding puns – jokes   14
Reading aloud   15

Unit 4: All in a Day
Reading/comprehension diary   16
Making notes from comic   17
Writing diary from notes   17
Anticipation activity   18
Making a chart of a perfect day   19

Unit 5: A Pantomime – writing for children
Listening to the pantomime   20
Comprehension – sequencing   21
Listening and remembering   22
Writing a character sketch   22
Writing part of a pantomime   23

Unit 6: Work it out
Anticipating a range of texts   24
Group problem solving   26

Unit 7: Views, Views, Views
Reading/comprehension article   28
Writing own article on TV   29
Reading Fast Forward letters page   30
Comprehension of letters   31
Discussion on effects of programmes   31
Writing a letter   31

Unit 8: Fair Play
Compiling words for description   32
Listening to Sound Effects tape   33
Writing description of fair   33
Drawing word sounds   33
Comprehension of text   34
Discussion   35
Making a radio programme   35

Unit 9: In the News
Cloze: Newspaper article   36
Writing/designing a Lost Notice   37
Writing a Newspaper article   37
Reading/anticipating – headlines   38
Matching headlines with articles   39

Unit 10: School Days
Listening, understanding story   40
Taking notes while listening   42
Writing character sketch   42
Writing story   42
Designing cover of book   42
Cloze. Poetry   43

Punctuation
Sentences   44
Question marks   45
Capital letters   46
Commas   47
Speech marks   48
Paragraphs   52

Spelling
1   First, final and middle letters   53
2   Short vowel patterns   54
3   Short vowels   55
4   Initial blends   56
5   Initial blends   57
6   Final blends   58
7   Plurals   59
8   Final 'e'   60
9   Final 'e'   61
10   Suffixing   62
11   Suffixing   63

Unit 1 People and Places

ACTIVITY 1: as a class

Read the chart below.

Name
Fred Aaron Savage

Date of birth
9 July 1976

Birth sign
Cancer

Height
1.47m (4ft 10in)

Weight
39kg (6st)

Hair
Brown

Eyes
Brown

Family details
Eldest of three children: sister Kala, brother Ben

Home
California

Hobbies
Playing sports, collecting baseball cards, reading

Favourite singers
Prince, Whitney Houston

Favourite food
Hot dogs

Favourite drink
Milk

Likes
The Chicago Bears football team

Dislikes
Having to babysit to earn pocket money

ACTIVITY 2: with a partner

Read the chart again.
Write down if the sentences below are
True (T) or **False (F)**, e.g.

1 = T

1 Fred has one brother and one sister.
2 His sister is called Karen.
3 She is older than him.
4 Fred was born in 1976.
5 He is twenty years old.
6 His birthday is on June 9th.
7 The food Fred likes best is hot baked potatoes.
8 His favourite drink is water.
9 One of Fred's hobbies is collecting baseball cards.
10 One of his other hobbies is playing sports.
11 Fred likes to babysit to earn pocket money.

ACTIVITY 3: with a partner or in a small group

What else would you like to find out about Fred Savage?
Work out some more facts you would like to see in his chart.

ACTIVITY 4: on your own

Plan a chart about yourself.
You can put down whatever facts you like.
Add a drawing or photograph of yourself.

ACTIVITY 5: on your own

You could also make a chart for a pet.
Here are some examples.

Pet's Choice

From: Sam the goose who belongs to Jayne Henry, age 11, Lisbellow

Food
Grass, bread

Drink
Water

Hobby
Running round a lot

Likes
Eating

Dislikes
Having a wash

Pet's Choice

From: Sooty the cat who belongs to Sunil Patel, age 13, Coventry

Favourite food
Fish

Favourite drink
Cream

Hobby
Trying to catch the fish in the bowl

Bad habit
Scratching the armchair

Good habit
Sitting on my bed

UNIT 1: PEOPLE AND PLACES

ACTIVITY 6: as a class or in a group

Listen to the sound effects tape.
Write down the sounds that you can hear.

ACTIVITY 7: as a class or in a group

Listen to the tape of the poem.
Listen again. Put up your hands each time the poem is about one of the sounds you heard in Activity 6.

Half Asleep
Half asleep
And half awake
I drift like a boat
On an empty lake.
And the sounds in the house
And the street that I hear
Though far away sound very clear.
That's my sister Betty
Playing by the stairs
Shouting like teacher
At her teddy bears.
I can hear Mum chatting
To the woman next door
And the tumble drier
Vibrates through the floor.
That's Alan Simpson
Playing guitar
While his Dad keeps trying
To start their car.
Dave the mechanic
Who's out on strike
Keeps revving and tuning
His Yamaha bike.
From the open window
Across the street
On the August air
Drifts a reggae beat.
At four o'clock
With a whoop and a shout
The kids from St John's
Come tumbling out.
I can hear their voices
Hear what they say
And I play in my head
All the games that they play.

by Gareth Owen

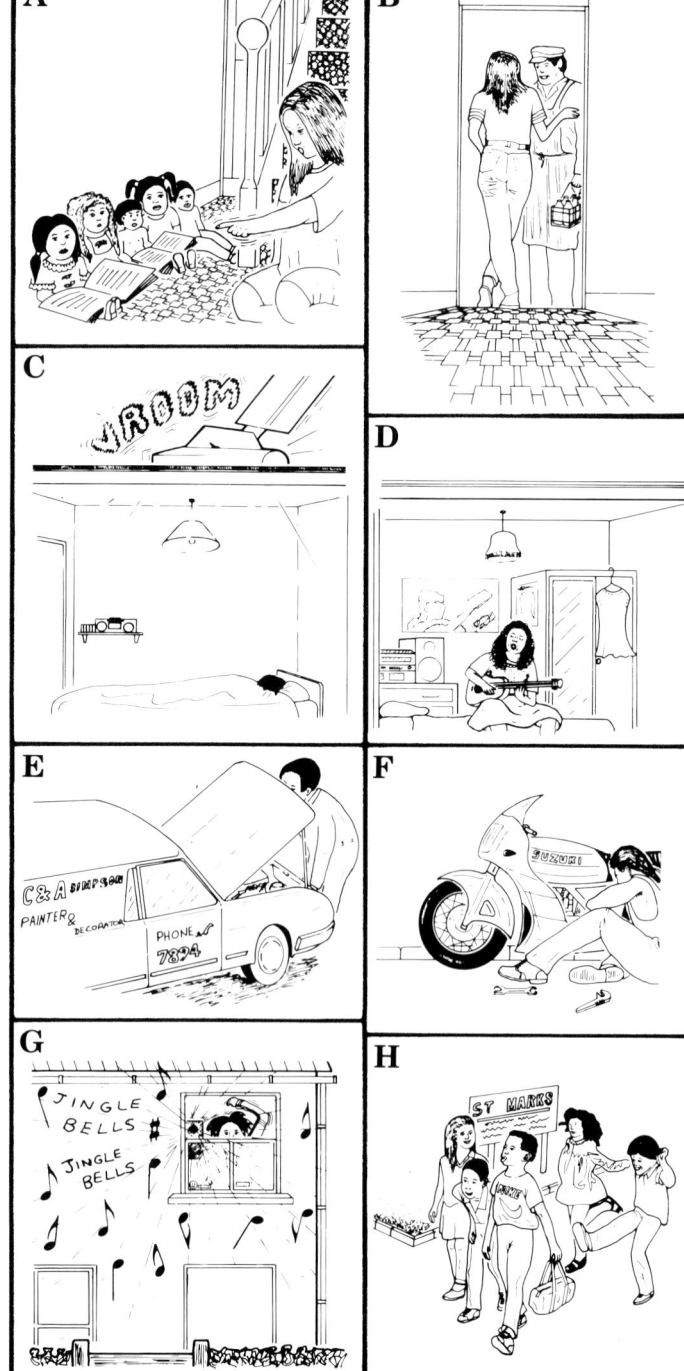

6   UNIT 1: PEOPLE AND PLACES

ACTIVITY 8: on your own or with a partner

The eight pictures **A–H** show some of the things that are happening in the poem.
In each picture, the artist has made **one** mistake.
Read the poem carefully and spot the mistakes.

ACTIVITY 9: as a class or in a group

Discuss the questions about the poem.

1 What day do you think the poem is describing?
2 How old do you think the person is who was 'half asleep'?
3 Is the place where you live, like this street? How is it different?
4 Which words in the poem describe sounds?
5 Do you like this poem? If you do, say why.

ACTIVITY 10: with a partner

One person has picture **A** (below).
The partner has picture (**a**) from the Teachers' Book (the other person must not see it).
The person with picture **A** describes it in detail.
The partner must listen carefully – picture **a** is different.
The partner marks picture (**a**) where there is a difference.
The partner must not ask questions.
Change roles for pictures **B** and (**b**).

UNIT 1: PEOPLE AND PLACES

Unit 2 Do's and Don'ts

🔊 ACTIVITY 1: as a class

Listen to the poem below a few times.
For each of the numbered sayings, discuss what sort of things might have been happening.

Irritating Sayings

Isn't it time you thought about bed?
It must be somewhere. [1]
You speak to him Harold, he won't listen to me.
Who do you think I am?
You'd better ask your father.
It's late enough as it is.
Don't eat with your mouth open.
In this day and age.
Did anyone ask your opinion? [2]
I remember when I was a boy.
And after all we've done for you.
You're not talking to your school friends now you know. [3]
Why don't you do it the proper way? [4]
I'm only trying to tell you.
What did I just say?
Now, wrap up warm.
B.E.D. spells bed.
Sit up straight and don't gobble your food.
For the five hundredth time.
Don't let me ever see you do that again. [5]
Have you made your bed?
Can't you look further than your nose? [6]
No more lip.
Have you done your homework?
Because I say so. [7]
Don't come those fancy ways here.
Any more and you'll be in bed. [8]
My, haven't you grown?
Some day I won't be here, then you'll see.
A chair's for sitting on. [9]
You shouldn't need telling at your age. [10]
Want, want want, that's all you ever say. [11]

collated by David Jackson

ACTIVITY 2: as a class

Think up all the sayings that irritate you.
Write your own class poem of irritating sayings.

ACTIVITY 3: as a class

Read your poem, each person taking a line.
Read your line with as much feeling as you can.

ACTIVITY 4: in small groups

Discuss what things irritate you most.

Y7 2022

My sister is always... nice

My Dad never... buy's me makeup

Whenever I want to watch... K-dramas my mum barges in

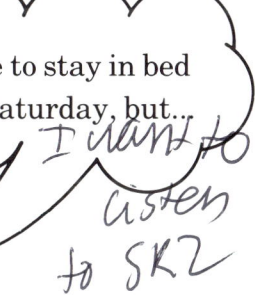

I like to stay in bed on Saturday, but... I want to listen to SKZ

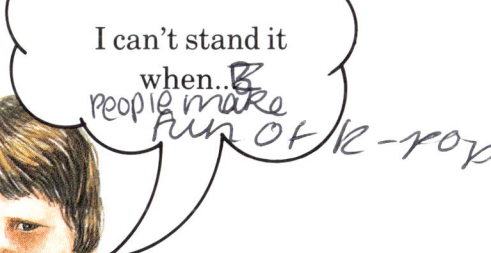

I can't stand it when... people make fun of K-pop

ACTIVITY 5: as a class

Make a tape recording of what people said in Activity 4.
Decide what order you are going to speak in.
Be ready to give your opinion when it is your turn.

ACTIVITY 6: with a partner

The paragraphs **A–G** are jumbled.
Put them into order so that they make sense, e.g.

The first paragraph = B

A
The tallest boy on the steps walked forward.
"Lead-in!" he shouted.
"Yes, Jeff," all the children said together.

B
Dinah walked on round the playground, waiting for the bell to ring or the whistle to go.

C
Still in silence, they began to march, row by row, up the steps and into the school. Their eyes were fixed in front of them and their feet kept in step. There was no giggling, or whispering or pushing. The only sound that you could hear was the tramping of feet.

D
"Yes, Rose," all the children said together. Then, like marching soldiers, they formed neat lines. Each child stood exactly a foot behind the one in front. Each line was exactly three feet from the one next to it. Not quite sure what to do, Dinah stood by herself.

E
There on the steps stood six children, three boys and three girls. They were all tall and they were all marked out from the others by a large white P on their blazer pockets. Without smiling, the tallest girl took a step forwards. "Form – rows!" she yelled into the silence.

F
But there was no bell. No whistle. Nothing. All the sounds in the playground just stopped and the children turned round to stare at the school.

G
Dinah stood still, watching, until the playground was almost empty. As the last line marched off, she tacked herself on to the end of it and walked towards the school. When she got to the top of the steps, Rose stuck out her arm.
"Name?" she asked briskly.
"Dinah Glass," Dinah said. "I'm new and..."

Adapted from "The Demon Headmaster" by Gillian Cross

ACTIVITY 7: with a partner

Look at the title of the story above.
What do you think the book is about?
What sort of things will happen when Dinah goes into the school?

ACTIVITY 8: as a class

Work out the key words that lead you from one paragraph to another, e.g.

paragraph 1 '... waiting for the bell...'
paragraph 2 '... there was no bell...'

ACTIVITY 9: on your own

Write a letter to someone who is going to come to your school.
Tell the new pupil:

- about the school uniform (boys' uniform and girls')
- what kit is needed for PE lessons
- what happens at the start of the school day
- how many break times there are
- what happens at lunch time
- how much homework there is

Set out your letter like the one on the right.

4 Ash Road,
Ayton,
Surrey,
SR1 4DJ.
2-6-92

Dear

Unit 3 Word Games

ACTIVITY 1: as a class and on your own

You are going to make a word game.
Your teacher will help you with material from the teachers' pack.

| c | e | n | a colour | an animal |

ACTIVITY 2: as a class or in a small group

Play the game.

ACTIVITY 3: on your own or with a partner

Give the game a name.
Make an instruction leaflet.

ACTIVITY 4: as a class

Listen to the poem opposite, a few times.
Then answer the questions on page 13.

The Computer's First Christmas Card

jollymerry
hollyberry
jollyberry
merryholly
happyjolly
jollyjelly
bellymerry
hollyheppy
jollyMolly
marryJerry
merryHarry
happyBarry
heppyJarry
boppyheppy
berryjorry
jorryjolly
moppyjelly
Mollymerry
Jerryjolly
bellyboppy
jorryhoppy
hollymoppy
Barrymerry
Jarryhappy
happyboppy
boppyjolly
jollymerry
merrymerry
merrymerry
merryChris
ammerryasa
Chrismerry
asMERRYCHR
YSANTHEMUM

by Edwin Morgan

Questions

1 Which words in the poem might be on a Christmas card?
2 Which words are names?
3 Some words are not real words, e.g. "jorry".
   a) Find five more words like that.
   b) What do each of these words sound as if they mean?
4 Find groups of words that rhyme, e.g. jolly, holly
5 Why do you think the poem is called "The Computer's First Christmas Card"?
6 How do you expect the poem to end?
7 Why do you think the poet made the ending different?

ACTIVITY 5: as a class

Prepare to write a poem that a computer makes, based on the word "lettergame".
Work out the words you can make by changing the first letter of the word "letter".
Do the same, changing the first vowel.
Now do the same with the word "name".
Discuss which words describe the game you played in Activity 2.

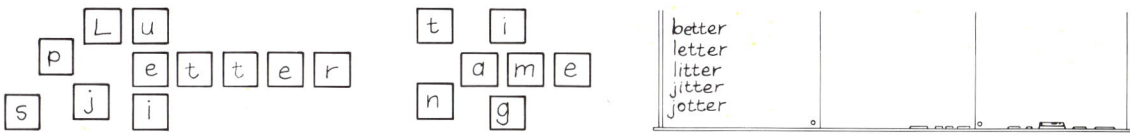

ACTIVITY 6: on your own

Write a poem that a computer makes about the game you played in Activity 2.
Pick the words you think best from the list you made in Activity 5.
Begin the poem: lettergame.

UNIT 3: WORD GAMES

ACTIVITY 7: in groups of three

In your group, number yourselves 1, 2 and 3.
Number 3 will need a copy of the blank outline **A**, below.
Number 1 has a copy of the complete picture, (**a**), in the Teacher's Book but must **not** show it to number 2 or 3.
Number 3 goes somewhere where she/he can't hear 1 and 2 talking.
Number 1 describes picture (**a**) to number 2.
Number 2 **listens** carefully then describes it, from memory, to number 3.
Number 3 fills in outline **A** as instructed by 2.
Now compare the picture number 1 has with the one number 3 has drawn.
Change places and do the same for the other two pictures, so that each person has a turn describing, remembering and listening.

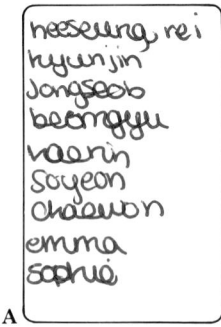
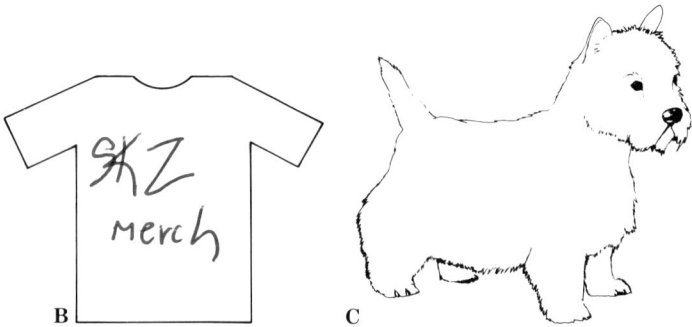

A   B   C

ACTIVITY 8: with a partner, in a small group or as a class

A pun is a play on words that sound alike, but have two different meanings.
Explain the puns in the jokes below.
Make a wall display of your own jokes with puns in them.

What do you get when you
cross a sheep with a kangaroo?
A woolly jumper.

What time do ducks get up?
At the quack of dawn.

Why didn't the chickens cost very much?
Because they were going cheap.

What do sea-monsters
eat for supper?
Fish and ships.

What do you call Batman and Robin
after they have run into a
steam-roller?
Flatman and Ribbon.

Why was six frightened
of seven?
Because seven ate nine.

Why was Cinderella rubbish at football?
Because her coach was a pumpkin.

Two flies were playing football in a saucer.
What did one say to the other?
We're playing in the cup next week.

UNIT 3: WORD GAMES

ACTIVITY 9: with a partner

Help each other to read aloud the poems below.
Try to make the meaning clear.
You could both read "Busy Day".
One could read the questions, the other, the answers.

Busy Day

Pop in
pop out
pop over the road
pop out for a walk
pop in for a talk
pop down to the shop
can't stop
got to pop

got to pop?

pop where?
pop what?

well
I've got to
pop round
pop up
pop in to town
pop out and see
pop in for tea
pop down to the shop
can't stop
got to pop

got to pop?

pop where?
pop what?

well
I've got to
pop in
pop out
pop over the road
pop out for a walk
pop in for a talk...

by Michael Rosen

YELLOW BUTTER

Yellow butter purple jelly red jam black bread

Spread it thick
Say it quick

Yellow butter purple jelly red jam black bread

Spread it thicker
Say it quicker
Yellow butter purple jelly red jam black bread

Now repeat it
While you eat it

Don't talk
With your mouth full!

by Mary Ann Hoberman

ACTIVITY 10: with a partner

Make a tape recording of the poem you like best.

UNIT 3: WORD GAMES

Unit 4 All in a Day

ACTIVITY 1: on your own or with a partner

Read Chris's diary.
Copy the boxes below.
Then fill in the boxes, using the details from the diary.

> Friday July 2nd
> Had quite a good day at school. Claire Fitt was sent home because they thought she had mumps, so we all went round pretending to have sore throats. Mark nearly fooled old Mrs Dixon into sending him home, until Helen Barnes grassed on him.
>   I got nine out of ten for my spelling which really pleased me, because for once I had really tried to learn them. I meant to tell Mum and Dad but when I got home I had a horrible shock. They're going away next week for FIVE DAYS. I ask you, FIVE DAYS! And guess who's coming to look after us. Granny Stokes.
>   So, it's going to be hell here next week. Horrible cooked dinners with piles of cabbage and Debbie getting all her own way.
>   I am pleased about one thing though. I have definitely grown out of that blue anorak Aunt Rose gave me last year. I showed it to Mum last night and even she had to agree it was too small. GREAT. I can buy a new one on Saturday.

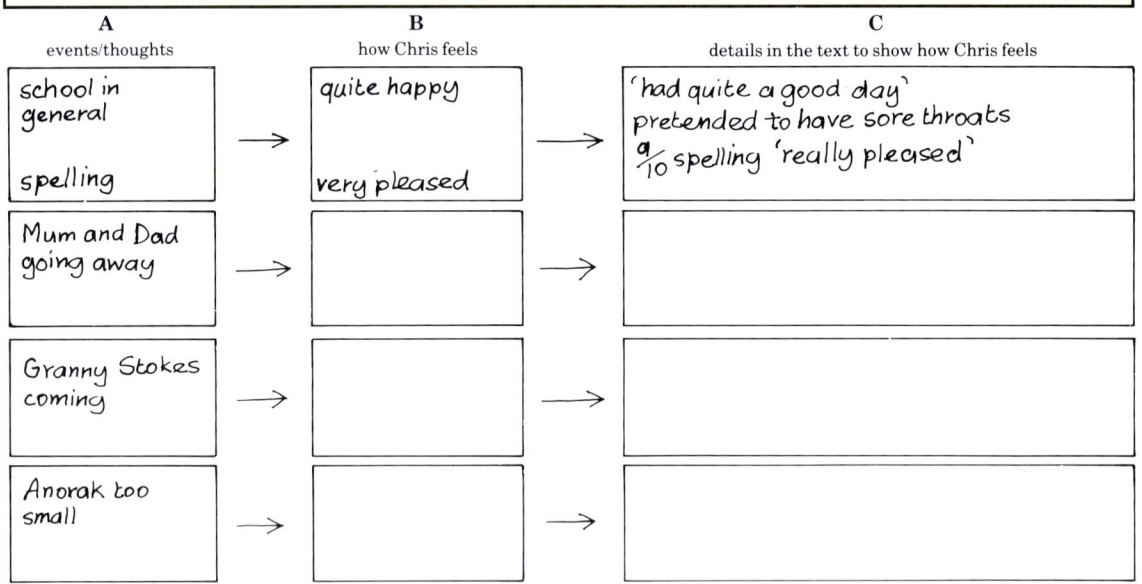

ACTIVITY 2: in small groups

Each person needs a copy of the boxes **A**, **B** and **C**.
Work on the first three pictures for July 6th opposite.

1 Write down the events/thoughts for July 6th in the boxes under **A**.
2 a) Discuss how Chris would feel about these events/thoughts (**B**).
  b) Discuss what you could put in the diary to make this clear (**C**).
  c) Using these ideas, fill in boxes **B** and **C**.
3 Discuss what other things could happen on July 6th.
   For each idea, fill in a box under **A**.

Do the same for the other set of pictures for July 19th.

ACTIVITY 3: on your own

Using the notes you made in Activity 2, write the three entries in Chris's diary, e.g.

> July 6th
> Good news at school. There's going to be a week's camping

UNIT 4: ALL IN A DAY

ACTIVITY 4: as a class

Start by reading the story below.
Each time you come to a row of dots, stop and discuss.

1 What will happen next?
2 Why do you think this?
3 Give your evidence, e.g. a word or phrase etc. from the text.

Curtis looked at the slip of paper and blushed.
"Will you come to my disco on Friday?" it said. "It starts at 7.30. Carla."
Curtis looked at the note again. There was a small kiss after her name.
Curtis blushed even more. He slipped the paper into his pocket, before Mr Smith spotted it. Then he waited for Carla to turn round.

....

"Why aren't you working, Curtis Skinner?" Mr Smith asked crossly.
"I am, Sir," Curtis said. "I was just thinking."
"Mmm, well don't strain yourself!" Mr Smith said.
One or two of the class giggled. Then Carla turned round and Curtis nodded.
"Curtis!" Mr Smith shouted. "If you haven't done your work by the end of this lesson, you will have to stay in after school."
Curtis bent over his book and tried to work.

....

"Bring your book up here, Curtis," Mr Smith said, at the end of the lesson.
"It was too hard, Sir," Curtis said, as he put his book on the desk.
"Rubbish!" Mr Smith snapped. "You are one of the best people at maths, in your year! See me in room twenty-six at 3.15."
Curtis opened his mouth to protest, but he knew it was no good.
"What you going to do?" Kevin asked at breaktime. "Your dad won't let you go to the disco, will he?"
"Not if he finds out I'm in detention tonight," Curtis said glumly.

....

Mr Smith handed Curtis the books, "I'll be back in half an hour," he said.

Curtis sat alone, listening to the clatter of the cleaners. All he could think about was how to get to the disco. He had three days to put his father in the right mood. But how? He could get the dinner ready at night and lay the table. But he did that most nights anyway. What else could he do?

Suddenly Curtis heard footsteps and the door was flung open.

....

"What's this?" Mr Smith said, when he looked at the books. "You've been here all this time and done nothing!"

For a moment, Curtis thought Mr Smith was going to burst. Then he seemed to calm down. "Anything wrong at home?" he asked suddenly, peering closely at Curtis.

Curtis shook his head.

"Right then," Mr Smith said, coldly. "Bring me this work at ten to nine, tomorrow. And do two extra pages. If you don't, I'll write to your father."

ACTIVITY 5: with a partner or in a small group

Discuss the different ways this story could end.

ACTIVITY 6: on your own

Pick the ending for the story about Curtis that you liked best.
Using this ending, write a few sentences to finish the story.

ACTIVITY 7: on your own or with a partner

Copy the chart below into your book but make yours bigger.
The chart is to give details of your idea of a perfect day.
Part of the chart has already been started, as an example.
Unless that is your idea of the perfect start to a day, you need not copy it.

THE PERFECT DAY

TIME	DETAILS
12 o'clock	Get up after a long lie in. No one nags about staying in bed.
12-10	Enormous breakfast, raid

Unit 5 A Pantomime – writing for children

ACTIVITY 1: as a class

Listen to the tape of the pantomime.
Say what you think will happen next. Give your reasons.
Read the script below and discuss how it compares with your answer.

JOHN TULLY   (Eating) If it wants any of this it will have to be sharp. Oh I am hungry.
  (Slowly, a FIZZWHIZZ head appears from the wings, makes a cuckoo noise and disappears.)
FIZZWHIZZ   Cuckoo.
JOHN TULLY   (Puzzled) Funny...
  (The FIZZWHIZZ appears from the other side and vanishes.)
FIZZWHIZZ   Cuckoo.
JOHN TULLY   Very funny
  (A FIZZWHIZZ head appears upside down, from the wings.)
FIZZWHIZZ   Cuckoo.
JOHN TULLY   (Still eating) It'll be a Fizzwhizz. I'll just ignore it.
  (The FIZZWHIZZ patters across the stage.)
FIZZWHIZZ   Cuckoo. Cuckoo.
JOHN TULLY   I'm not going to look at it. I'm having nothing to do with it.
  (The FIZZWHIZZ hops round JOHN TULLY then sits at his feet.)
FIZZWHIZZ   Hello. I'm the Fizzwhizz.
JOHN TULLY   (Not looking at it) I know. Go away. I don't want you.
FIZZWHIZZ   All right. I'll go.
  (The FIZZWHIZZ starts going away quickly.)

JOHN TULLY	There you are. You just have to be firm with them.
FIZZWHIZZ	(From off stage) I've gone!
FIZZWHIZZ	(From further away) I've gone!
FIZZWHIZZ	(Very loudly, over the loud speakers) I'VE GONE!
JOHN TULLY	Oh, I wish it would leave me alone.
	(The FIZZWHIZZ patters back and sits at JOHN TULLY'S feet.)
FIZZWHIZZ	(Sweetly) I'm the Fizzwhizz.
JOHN TULLY	I know you're the Fizzwhizz. I can see you're the Fizzwhizz, but I don't want you around. Go AWAY!
FIZZWHIZZ	(Bursting into tears and howling) Wah-wah-wah-wah.
JOHN TULLY	Oh dear. I'm sorry I didn't mean...
FIZZWHIZZ	Wah-wah-wah-wah.
JOHN TULLY	Oh dear. Don't get upset. Look. Have this bread and honey.
	(The FIZZWHIZZ stops crying, grabs the sandwich and starts eating happily.)

From 'John Tully and the Bee People' by Allan Cullen.

ACTIVITY 2: with a partner, or on your own

The pictures below show what is happening in the pantomime.
Read the pantomime again carefully and put the pictures in the right order.

UNIT 5: A PANTOMIME – WRITING FOR CHILDREN

ACTIVITY 3: as a class

Discuss these questions.

1. Why was the Fizzwhizz being such a pest?
2. Why do you think the Fizzwhizz got its way in the end?
3. What do you think young children would like best about this part of the pantomime?

ACTIVITY 4: as a class

Listen to the rest of the tape.
Discuss the questions below.

1. Why was Humble cross with John Tully?
2. Where do John Tully and Humble want to go?
3. Why can't they get there?
4. Humble says that the Fizzwhizz is brainless. What do you think?
5. What sort of character is the Fizzwhizz?
6. What would young children like best about this part of the pantomime?

ACTIVITY 5: on your own or with a partner

Write a small character sketch of a Fizzwhizz for someone who has no idea what kind of character it is.
In your writing, answer the questions below.

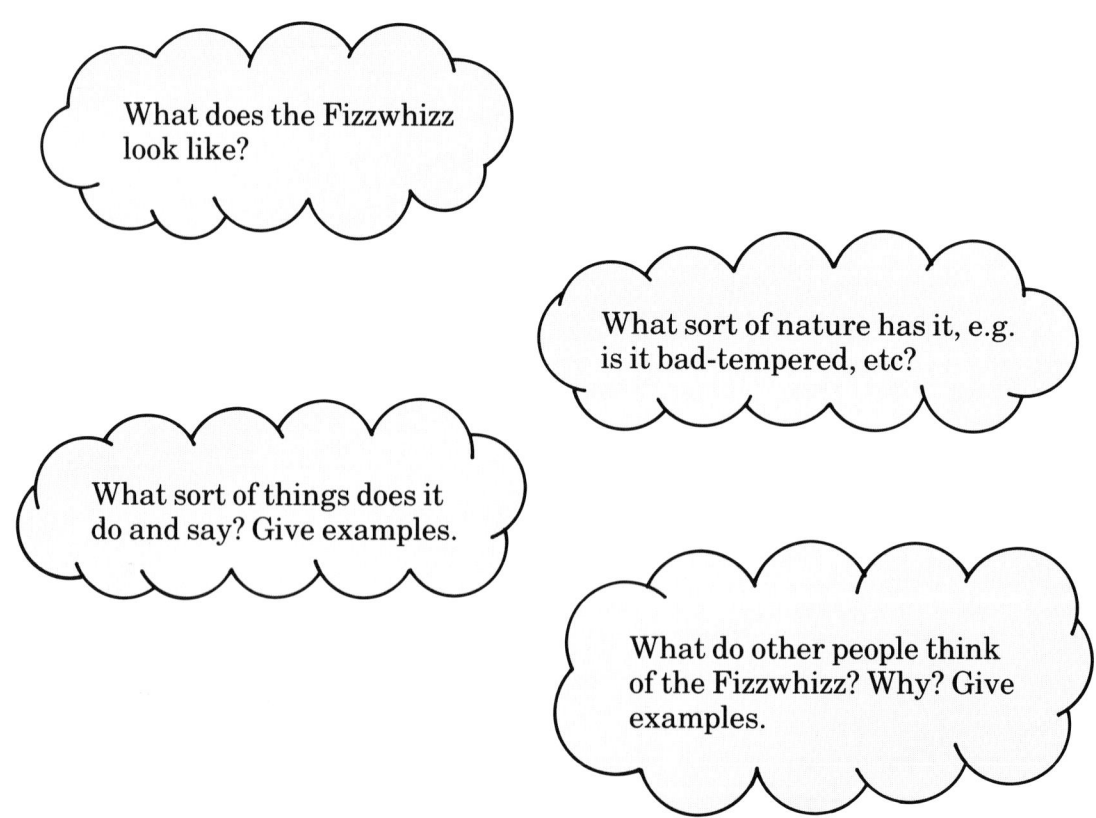

ACTIVITY 6: as a class or in small groups

The picture above shows the dungeons in the Paper Palace.
The princess is being kept a prisoner by the wicked Beadle.
John Tully and the Fizzwhizz are coming to the rescue.
Discuss the things that might happen in this part of the pantomime.
Remember to think about:

- what sort of things young children will like best
- how the Fizzwhizz will behave

ACTIVITY 7: with a partner or as a class

Pick the part of the rescue scene (from Activity 6) that you like best.
Write down this part of the scene.
In your final draft remember the points below.

Unit 6 Work it out

ACTIVITY 1: with a partner or in a group

A-D are all extracts from books.
Read **A** carefully and work out:

- what you think happened in the story, just before this extract
- what you think will happen just after the extract

Do the same for **B** and **D**.
With **C**, work out what was said before and after this extract.

A Ray had put the snails side by side on a narrow, foot-long sheet of glass. For a moment Gary couldn't think where he'd seen it before; then he remembered – and looked at the dressing table. That, indeed, was where it had come from. He grinned as he thought of what his mother would say if she could see what was going on. No wonder Ray had told him to lock the door.

   At the other end of the glass "running track", Ray put down the scrap of cabbage.

Adapted from "In the Net" by Michael Hardcastle

B He ran home to his wife and gave her the ring.
"Oh where did you get it?" He said not a thing.
"It's the loveliest ring in the world," she said,
As it glowed on her finger. They skipped off to bed.
At midnight they woke. In the dark outside,
"Give me my ring!" a chill voice cried.
"What was that, William? What did it say?"
"Don't worry, my dear. It'll soon go away."
"I'm coming!" A skeleton opened the door.
"Give me my ring!" It was crossing the floor...

From "The Visitor" by Ian Serraillier

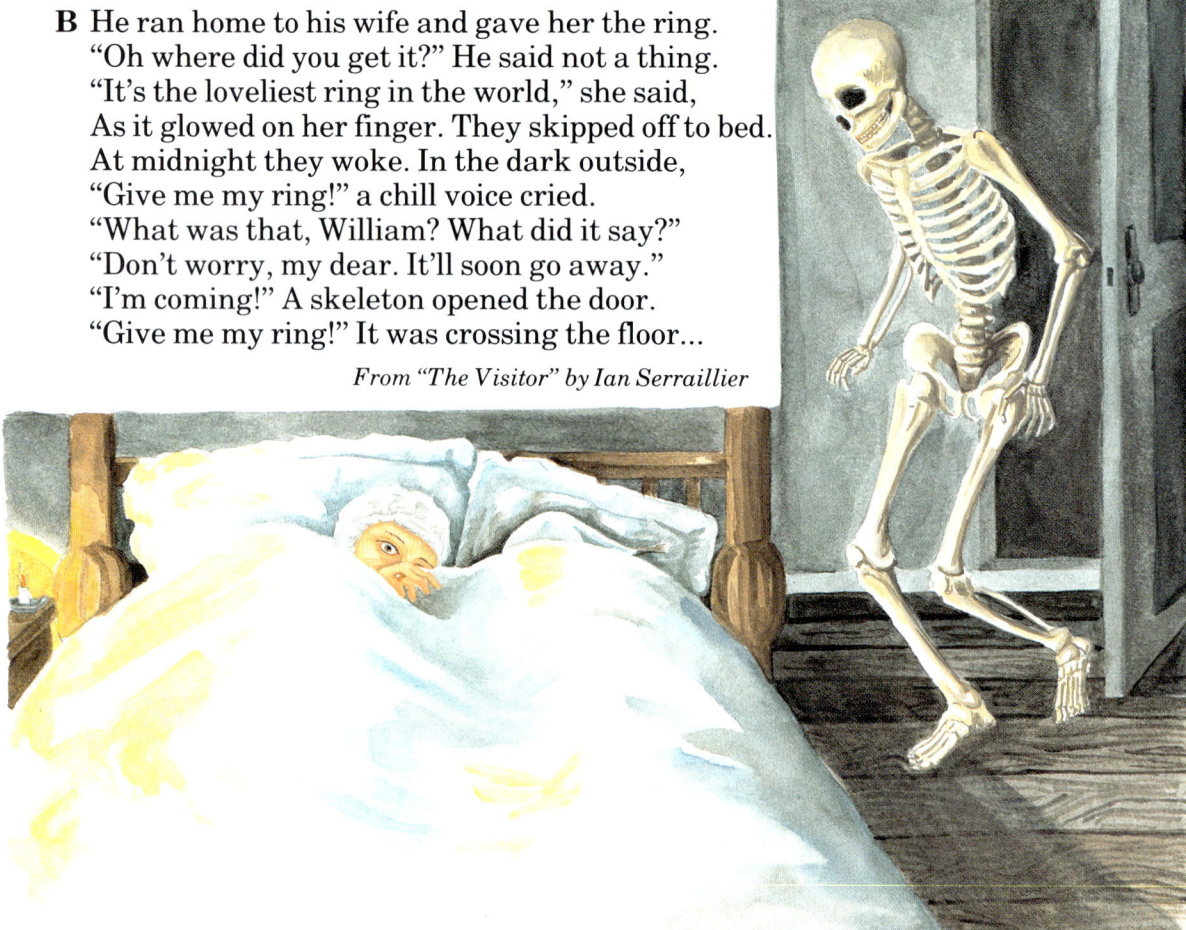

Fig 1

Fig 2

Fig 3

C When the cards are dry, fold them in half and glue them together (Fig 1). Now glue the back onto the other two halves (Fig 2).

Now you will have a card with a flap that moves (Fig 3). It can show a nine of Clubs or a Jack of Spades.

To do the trick, hold the card in your right hand with the flap upwards...

Adapted from "Amaze and Amuse Your Friends," by Peter Eldin

D "I don't see what you're moaning about," said Gran. "You wanted to help."

"I didn't want to *help*," I said. "I wanted to *offer* to help. The two are not the same. And also I didn't think I'd be washing up every plate ever made in the history of plate-making."

"Don't answer back," said Gran. "And there's some food still left on that plate there."

"Where?" I said.

Gran pointed to a plate at the very bottom of the stack. Have you ever noticed that the one people want is always at the bottom of the pile?

"It looks alright to me," I said. I nearly added: Germs have got to eat too, but thought it was safer not to.

"Wash it again," said Gran.

So I did. Or, at least, I went to. The trouble was...

Adapted from "Bad Boyes" by Jim and Duncan Eldridge

ACTIVITY 2: in groups of three or four

Read everything in the box below.
Study **A–F** very carefully.
Then answer questions **1–3**.

> The girl in the picture at the top of the page, went away for a few days' holiday. When she got home her mother gave her anorak away for a jumble sale.
>
> The girl who bought the anorak found some things still in the pocket. The more the girl looked at the things, the more she found out about the girl and the first day of her holiday. See how much you can find out.

Questions

1. Use the map to work out the journey Laura made on the first day of her holiday. Then mark on your map the journey that **D** was used for.
2. Where did the person who wrote the letter probably live? What might her relationship be to Laura?
3. Work out Laura's movements from the time she left home.

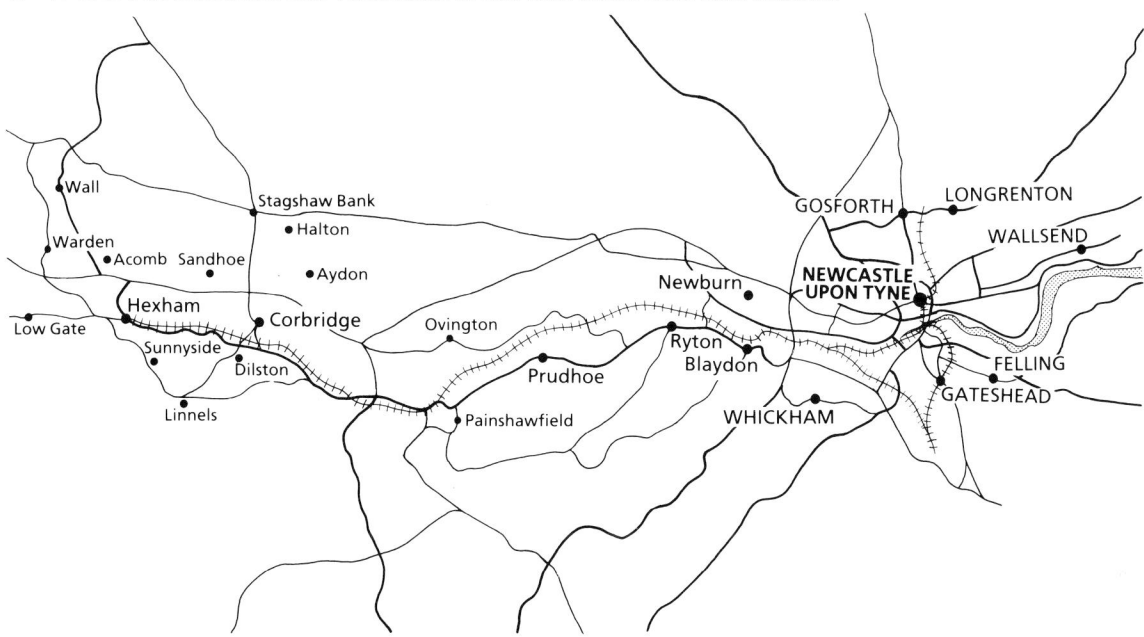

UNIT 6: WORK IT OUT

Unit 7 Views, Views, Views

WHAT I WATCH

Carol Vorderman, maths wizard of C4's 'Countdown', admits to being a TV addict.

I love TV and if I had the chance I think I would watch it all day. It's just as well that I have so much work that I haven't the time.

I've only one TV, but when I'm at home, it's always on. If it was up to me I would have one in every room in the house, the bathroom as well; but my family won't let me.

If I could watch one programme, then it would be 'Coronation Street'. I love it. There is nothing else like it. One minute you are sitting on the edge of your chair, hardly daring to breathe. Next you are helpless with laughter.

I think it is the best programme because the people in it are nice. You can't say that about 'EastEnders', which I don't watch. In fact I don't watch any other soaps.

I do watch the news as often as I can, as I don't have time to read the papers. I usually watch 'News at Ten' and 'ITN News at 5.40'.

For something quite different, 'Blind Date' takes some beating. It is so funny. I feel a bit embarrassed when the people in it try to be funny; but most of the time they are just themselves. As for Cilla Black, I don't think anyone else could do it so well. She is everyone's big sister.

Whenever I can, I spend Saturday afternoons with C4 watching black-and-white films from the 30s and 40s. I love the weepy ones, with stars like Bette Davis and Joan Crawford.

ACTIVITY 1: on your own or with a partner

Read the article from the "TV Times."
Copy the chart below, but make yours bigger.
Fill in the rest of the chart using the details from the article.

Programme	Reasons for liking it	Reasons for not liking it
Coronation Street		
EastEnders		

ACTIVITY 2: on your own or with a partner

Write down the first word of each of the sentences in the article on page 28.
How many different words are there?
What is the effect of having different words?

ACTIVITY 3: on your own

Make a list of your favourite television programmes.
Make a list of your least favourite programmes.
Now make a chart like the one on page 28.
Give as many reasons for liking, or not liking, a programme as you can.

ACTIVITY 4: on your own

Using the details in your chart, write your own article about what **you** watch.
Plan your article first. The checklist of the main points in Carol Vorderman's article may help you.
In the final draft, set out your article like the one on page 28.

Remember: try to make some of your sentences start with different words.
put the title of programmes in inverted commas, e.g.

inverted commas — ' EastEnders ' — *inverted commas*
capital letter

The main points in Carol Vorderman's article
- Feelings about television – how many hours spent watching it.
- If she could only watch one programme, what it would be and why.
- The programmes she does not like and why.
- The programmes she likes, with reasons.
- Her favourite day for watching TV and why.

Lettuce Page

This letters section gives you the chance to have a say about the mag, television, radio or anything else. We'll give a Lorus Quartz watch to the person who writes the best letter of the week.

If you have been watching the news, you will know about the terrible drought in Ethiopia. It really made me think how lucky we are to live here, where there is no fighting and no one is starving.

Angela Exmouth

(Well done Angela. It's nice to know that people still care about others who are not as lucky as ourselves. A watch is on its way to you - Editor)

My brother is three. Before he watched the 'Teenage Mutant Heroes', he was nice, but now he isn't. It is because of the violence in the cartoon. The turtles throw things at Shredder. My brother keeps on attacking me and my sisters saying, 'I'll get you Shredder'.

Redcar

I think 'Grange Hill' is good. It teaches us about things and it shows us what to do if we ever get into a fight. As for things like animal rights, it helps to get young people involved.

Glasgow

I feel sad because the turtle craze has made people buy terrapins without even thinking about their needs. I watched 'Newsround' and saw that lots of children didn't know how to feed them. I love terrapins and I hate to see them not looked after properly.

Belgium

I think 'Grange Hill' sets a very bad example to children growing up. The children in the programme are very rude to the teachers and talk back. It is very violent at times. It makes me scared of going to a comprehensive school.

Katie James

FAST FORWARD address
Fast Forward, PO Box 114
Leatherhead, Surrey, KT22 9DG

ACTIVITY 5: with a partner or as a class

Read the "Lettuce Page" on page 30.
Answer the questions below.

Questions
1 Who wrote the best letter of the week?
2 Why do you think that particular letter was picked?
3 What sort of watch was sent to the writer of the best letter?
4 Why do you think the editor wrote her comments in italics?
5 Why do you think the page is called "Lettuce Page"?

ACTIVITY 6: on your own or with a partner

Copy the form below but make yours bigger.
Read the letters in the "Lettuce Page" again.
Write down the names of the programmes discussed in the letters.
Next to each name, write down the views of the letter writers.

Name of programme	Good effects of programme	Bad effects of programme
'News' and 'News round'		
'Teenage Mutant Heroes'		

ACTIVITY 7: as a class or in a group

Now discuss the programmes you like and dislike most.
Write the names of these programmes down.
Write your views on these programmes in the same way that you did in Activity 6.

ACTIVITY 8: on your own

Write a letter about a programme.
Say whether you think the programme has good effects, or not.
You could make your own "Lettuce Pages" or send your letters to the Fast Forward address which is at the bottom of page 30.

Unit 8 Fair Play

ACTIVITY 1: with a partner

Look at the picture of the fair.
Write down all the things that you see at a fair.
Make a list on the left-hand side of the page, e.g.

1 candyfloss
2 darts

Add to your list any other things you might see at a fair, which are not in the picture.

ACTIVITY 2: with a partner

Write a few words to describe each object in your list.
Use the questions below to help you.

1 What does it look like?
2 How does it move?
3 What does it taste like?
4 What does it feel like?
5 Any other details.

Write down your ideas next to your words.

1 candyfloss – sticky, sweet, pink, sticks to face
2 darts – whizzing, flash of silver

ACTIVITY 3: with a partner

Listen to the tape of a fair.
As you listen, see how many different sounds you can hear.
Listen to the tape again, and this time list all the sounds that you hear.
Write them down on the left-hand side of your paper, e.g.

1 screams

Add to your list any other sounds you might hear at a fair.

ACTIVITY 4: with a partner

Write a few words to describe each sound, e.g.

1 screams – of fear, terror

ACTIVITY 5: on your own

Use the notes that you have made in Activities 1 – 4.
Write a description of a fairground at night.
Try to write so that someone who has never been to a fair, can almost **feel** and **hear** what it is like.

ACTIVITY 6: with a partner or in a small group

Some words can be made to look a little like their meaning.
Write down some other words like the ones below.
Make a wall display.

UNIT 8: FAIR PLAY

"Why can't I¹ go to the fair tonight?" Lisa asked crossly.

Mrs West sighed. "Lisa we² have this every year," she³ said. "You⁴ are too young."

"You⁵ always say that!" Lisa shouted. "I'm twelve now, remember? Not eleven or ten."

"Don't be rude, love," Mrs West said, putting down her⁶ fork. "You don't really think I'm going to let you walk round a place like that, on your own at night, do you?"

"I'm not going on my own, am I?" Lisa shouted. "Ann and Clare are going with me and they're only eleven."

"I don't care if they⁷ are nine," Mrs West said firmly. "If you want to go so badly, go with them⁸ in the afternoon, or I'll go with you in the evening."

"Oh come on, Mum," Lisa said. "No one goes with their mum at my age. And what would you⁹ do with Carl and Tom anyway?"

Mrs West shook her head. "I don't know Lisa. I do my best. I let you stay up until half past nine in the week and go to discos at the weekend. That's more than Sara Betts can do, because her¹⁰ mother told me¹¹."

ACTIVITY 7: on your own

Read the story above.
Each of the underlined words refers to a person or people.
Work out who they are.
Use the list to help you, e.g. 1 = C

The list
A Ann and Clare
B Mrs West
C Lisa
D Sara Betts
E Mrs West and Lisa

ACTIVITY 8: on your own or with a partner

Read the story again.
Say which people in the story **might** have said 1 – 4 below.

1 "Sara! Switch that off and go to bed. It's nine o'clock."
2 "Would you be able to baby-sit? Oh lovely. Yes. They're six and eight."
3 "I didn't go in the end, because Clare was sick."
4 "It was great. I went with Carly. And Mum just kept in the background."

ACTIVITY 9: in small groups

Discuss what you feel about the comments in the speech bubbles below.
You may have more views about how old you should be before you are allowed to do things, e.g. wear ear-rings, make-up, dye your hair.

ACTIVITY 10: as a class or in groups

Make a five minute radio programme, based on the discussion you had in Activity 9.

Give it a title, e.g. **Points of View**.
Plan how you will make the programme. You will need:

- **an announcer**: to give the title of the programme.
- **a presenter**: to say what the points of view are about.
  to say the name of the school and the class giving the opinions.
- **people**: ready to give their points of view.

  Decide on the order that you are going to speak in.
  Be ready to give your opinions when it is your turn.
  A teacher and other adults could join in.

UNIT 8: FAIR PLAY

Unit 9 In the News

No Problem Picking Out Speedy

Police had a shock when they spotted a tortoise rushing along the M6. The tortoise, 25 year-old Speedy, was on her way to Birmingham, on the inside lane.

Police took —1— to a home for lost pets, in Pershore Road. Soon 13 —2— old Paul Dunn came to pick her up. That was when the problems started. Other children who had lost their tortoises, —3— that Speedy was their pet too. So Paul had to —4— Speedy belonged to him.

It did not take more than a —5—. Speedy, who was with five other tortoises, had a dent in her shell.

Paul missed an afternoon's —6— to check up on his tortoise. The Headteacher —7— Saint Edmund Campion School, in Sutton Coldfield, let him have time off to look for his pet.

'Paul's tortoise went —8— two weeks ago,' said his mother, Mrs Eileen Dunn of Brookville Lane, Erdington. 'We put —9— up in all the shops nearby but we had given up hope of —10— her.'

'Speedy was always galloping off' Paul said.

Adapted from "The Birmingham Post"

ACTIVITY 1: with a partner

Read the article above.
Fill each gap with one word only.
Make sure it all makes sense.
Discuss the different words that could be used in some of the gaps, e.g.

9 = posters, or notices

ACTIVITY 2: on your own

When something is lost, people put up a poster like the one below.
Design the poster Mrs Dunn may have made when Speedy went missing.
Use the details from the article that need to go on the poster.

ACTIVITY 3: in a group

- Discuss the pets that you have.
- How could you tell your pet from five others of the same sort?
- Do you know anyone with unusual pets?

ACTIVITY 4: on your own

Write an article about someone who finds his/her lost pet.
The article is for a local daily newspaper.
The details can be true or made up.
Make a list of these details before you begin, e.g.

Dog – Tim, ten years old, mongrel, etc.

Now make a **plan** of your article.
You could use the plan from the article about Paul.

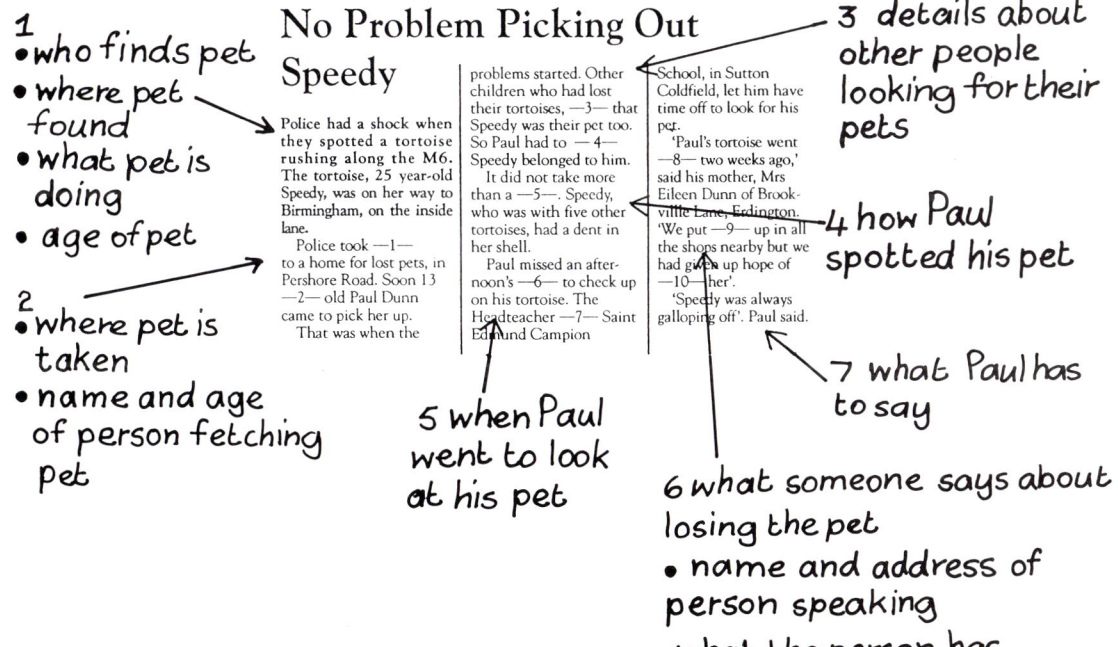

UNIT 9: IN THE NEWS   37

ACTIVITY 5: on your own

Work out how you are going to set out your work, e.g.

- write your article in three columns, as on page 36
- draw a picture or put in a photograph for your article
- give your article a headline (you might like to add this later, after Activities 6, 7 and 8)
- use one of the newspaper layouts below, or make up one of your own.

Try to make your article look as much like a newspaper article as possible.

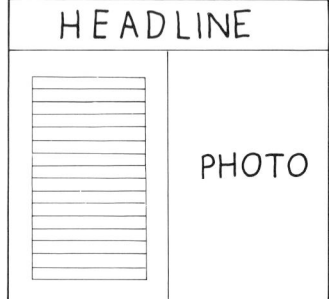
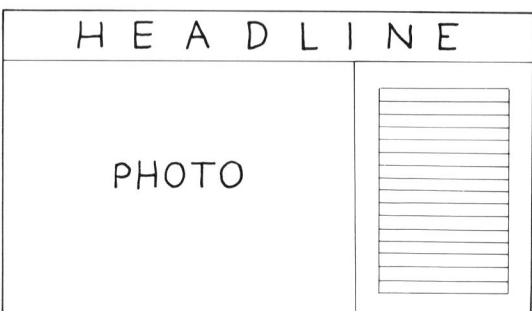
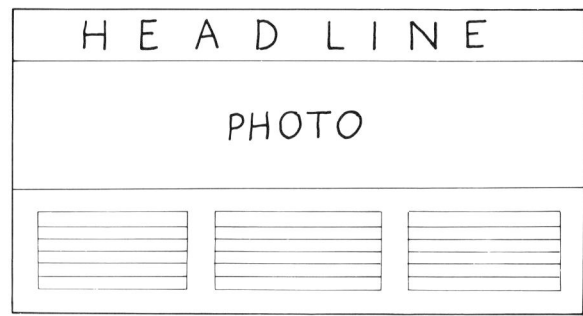
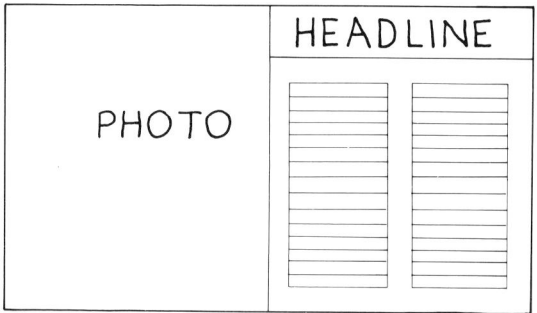

ACTIVITY 6: with a partner or in a small group

Read the headlines **A–G**.
Work out what you think the article for each headline might have been about.
One person can jot down the ideas.

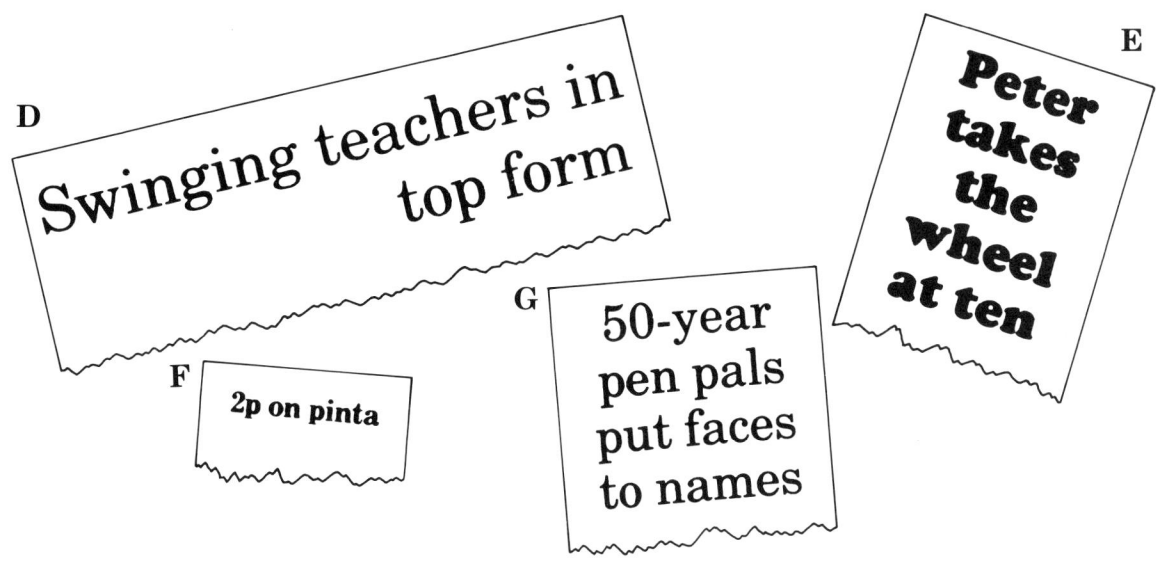

D Swinging teachers in top form

E Peter takes the wheel at ten

F 2p on pinta

G 50-year pen pals put faces to names

ACTIVITY 7: with a partner or on your own

Match each of the extracts 1–7, below with the correct headline, e.g.

A = 2

1 Andrew cunning whisked 17 year old bride to a on a JCB which he borrowed from his boss.

2 his cartoons are very good indeed and he is beginning to make a name for himself.

3 Milk could rise by as much as 2p a pint in October because the

4 He is getting used to the feel of a car and its controls after joining the Under Seventeens Car Club.

5 The group doesn't rock around the clock, but does spend a lot of time playing at school fund-raising discos.

6 As the boat sank, they grabbed fishing rods and got into a rubber life-boat

7 "You write to someone all your life and then suddenly you're standing right next to them.
"It's an experience you can't believe," said Mrs Mohler.

ACTIVITY 8: as a class

Are any of your answers different from the answers in Activity 6?
Why? What clues did you use? Were there any words that misled you?

UNIT 9: IN THE NEWS

Unit 10 School Days

🗅 ACTIVITY 1: as a class

Listen to the story.

ACTIVITY 2: as a class, with a partner or on your own

Read the extract from the story.
Then check how much you can remember by answering the questions opposite.

A boy had his hand up.

"Sir, that's not fair sir, because Booth isn't here, sir. He might know."

Mr Harmer moaned a long moan.

5   "We'll see then. In Booth's mighty brain lies the fate of Class Four's games lesson. We shall ask him if, and I stress if, he returns."

He turned to look at me for the first time.

"Where shall we put you? We're a bit short of room at the moment. Would you mind sitting next to Penelope, until we have a think what to
10   do with you?"

The class laughed and whistled. I was red enough to blow up. All the kids were grinning and pulling faces, and Mr Harmer was saying:

"Alright. That will do, that will do."

The space was right at the back of the room. Penelope turned away
15   from me and squashed herself to the other end of the bench. Mr Harmer said:

"I'm sure Penelope will look after you, won't you Penelope?"

She was as red as me. She had a white fluffy cardigan and long, brown wavy hair. I sat and stared down at the desk top. My eyes were
20   full of tears, and I breathed deeply to stop myself crying. At last a boy came round with some paper and pens and I could start writing, and once I could get on with that, it was almost the same as being at my old school.

From "The Big Red Apple" by Hamish Whiteley

How much can you remember?

Questions
1 What "wasn't fair"? (line 2)
2 What might Booth "know"? (line 3)
3 What does Mr Harmer say will happen, if Booth doesn't "know"?
4 "We shall ask him if he returns". (line 6)
   a) "Returns" from where?
   b) What has Booth been doing and why?
5 Why do you think the boy in the story is upset?

ACTIVITY 3: as a class, with a partner or on your own

Now do the same with this next extract.

Back in the class Mr Harmer asked me what had happened; I told him that I'd fallen over.
"Not over Mr Booth's foot, I hope. He does have a habit of leaving them lying about in the play ground."
I said it wasn't over Booth's foot and Mr Harmer said I could go and sit down.
On my desk was a piece of paper folded over. On the front it said, ...

Check your memory.

Questions
1 What had happened in the playground and why?
2 Why do you think the new boy in the story didn't tell Mr Harmer the truth?
3 What do you think Booth will think of the new boy? Say why.
4 Can you remember what was on the front of the note and inside the note?
5 Who do you think the note was from? Say why you think this.
6 How do you think the new boy is going to fit in to his new school? Say why think this.

ACTIVITY 4: as a class or with a partner

Jot down all that you know about Booth from:
- what he does
- what he says
- what other people think of him.

Now listen to the story again and add any more details.

What Booth does	What Booth says	What people think of Booth
Sticks his tongue out		

ACTIVITY 5: on your own

Using your notes to help you, write down what Booth was like to know.

ACTIVITY 6: on your own

Write a story about the day you started something new, e.g. a first day at a new school, or holiday camp, or club.

ACTIVITY 7: on your own

Design the cover for a book of short stories.
Put the title of "The Big Red Apple", or your own story, on the front.
Design a picture for the title story.
Write a few sentences about the title story for the back of the cover.
You could plan your cover like the one below.

Winter

On winter mornings in the playground
The boys stand huddled
Their cold hands —**1**—
Into trouser pockets.
The air hangs —**2**—
About the buildings
And the cold is an —**3**— in the blood
A pain on the tender skin
Beneath finger nails.
The odd shouts
Sound off like struck iron
And the sun
—**4**— white
Above the boundary wall.
I —**5**— my bus ticket
Between my —**6**— fingers
Into a fag,
Take a drag
And blow —**7**—
Into the December air.

by Gareth Owen

ACTIVITY 8: with a partner or in a group

Read the poem above.
Discuss the words that could be put in the gaps.

ACTIVITY 9: as a class or in a group

Compare your words with the words the poet chose.
Discuss the merits of each of the words.

Punctuation
Sentences

ACTIVITY 1: on your own or with a partner

A sentence must make sense and be complete, e.g.

The black cat	The black cat is very old
not complete	complete

Some of the groups of words below are not complete.
Write down the sentences only. **Remember**:

capital letter ⟶ The black cat is very old. ⟵ full stop

1. I am too hot
2. The black and white cat
3. The dog ran across the road
4. We walk to school in the morning
5. I go to bed at about ten o'clock
6. There is someone at the door
7. In time for tea
8. Six o'clock at night
9. Eggs, chips, baked beans and bread
10. I have got to go to the dentist

ACTIVITY 2: on your own or with a partner

Complete the groups of words below to make six sentences.
Use the picture to help you.
Remember: use a capital letter at the beginning and a full stop at the end.

1. The baby is _____
2. _____ are going to come crashing down
3. The boy and the girl _____
4. _____ is rushing to help
5. An old woman has _____
6. Two children are _____

Question marks

ACTIVITY 1: on your own

A question mark is put at the end of a question.
The "question" words on the right often start a question.
Work out which of the sentences below are questions.
Write out the questions in your book.
Remember: put a question mark at the end of each question.

1 It costs a pound to go on the outing
2 I wish I was a year older
3 When can I go to the disco
4 We usually do all the shopping on Friday night
5 Who is that boy over there
6 Why can't we have longer holidays
7 Dad wants to win the pools
8 How much pocket money do you get
9 I hate getting up when it is dark outside
10 Which card do you like best
11 Where are my shoes
12 That football is no good

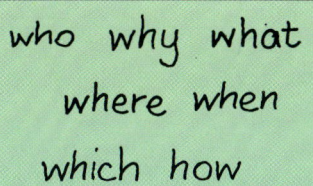

who why what
where when
which how

ACTIVITY 2: on your own

Turn the sentences below into questions.
Do not add or take away any words.
Just change the order of the words, e.g.

1 It is snowing → Is it snowing?

1 It is snowing.
2 You have got my rubber.
3 This sum is too hard.
4 The cat has gone upstairs.
5 Jason has gone to the dentist.
6 There are some tins on the shelf.
7 We can come at six o'clock.
8 That was the girl we saw last night.

ACTIVITY 3: on your own or with a partner

Below are a list of answers.
Write down the questions that were asked to get the answers below.
Remember: put a question mark at the end of each question.

Answers
1 I am twelve years old.
2 Mr Choudrey lives at number 14.
3 I've only got four pence.
4 I go to High Cross School.
5 I like PE best.
6 His name is Rex.
7 It takes about an hour a night.
8 We have a hamster and a cat.
9 Turn right and then left.
10 Yes, please.

Capital letters

ACTIVITY 1: on your own

Look at the picture below.
Write down all the times that capital letters are used.
By each set of words, write why capital letters are used, e.g.

1 *Avis Stores – name of a shop*

ACTIVITY 2: on your own

Write eight sentences about the picture above.
In each sentence use some of the words beginning with capital letters, e.g.

The boy's bike is a Raleigh

Remember: if you want to write the name of the book in your sentence, write it like this: "The Snowman".

ACTIVITY 3: on your own

Write about yourself or make up someone to write about.
You could use the chart you made on page 5 to help you.
You could include:

- your name
- age, date of birth
- where you live: road, town, county
- favourite pop stars, film stars
- name of best friends, pets, hobbies
- name of school you go to, the subjects you like best

Underline in colour, or highlight, all the words beginning with capital letters.
Remember: use capital letters at the beginning of sentences.
             try to use different words to start your sentences.

Commas

ACTIVITY 1: on your own

You use commas when you make a list.
Write three sentences listing some of the objects in **A–C** below.
Remember:
The cat screeched as plates, cups, knives and forks crashed onto the floor.

Commas come after each word in a list.   *no comma before 'and'.*

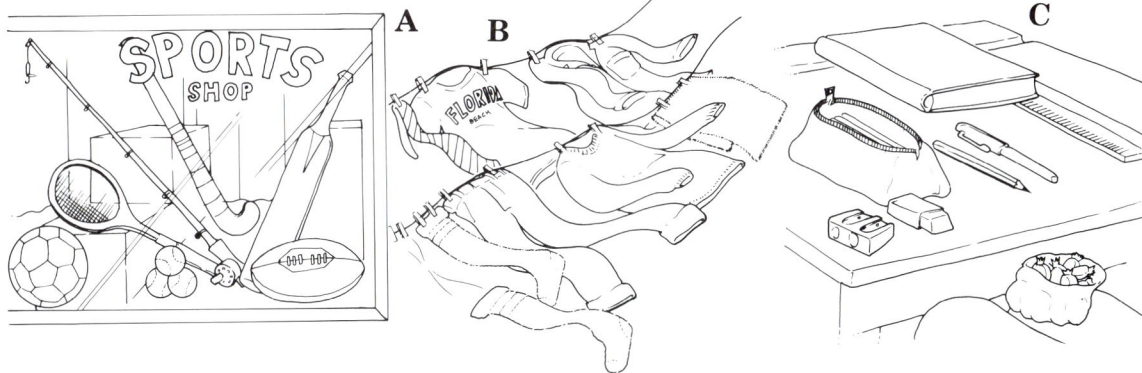

ACTIVITY 2: on your own

Write four more sentences listing objects.
You could write about:

- the food you like (or hate)
- things you like doing most
- the people you would most like to meet, etc.

ACTIVITY 3: on your own

Commas are used for writing an address.
Draw two envelopes in your book.
Write out the name and address for **B** and **C**.
Be careful, some commas are missing.
Use picture **A** to help you.

B

WRITE TO US
If you want to raise an Issue, please write to: Readers Write,
Athletics Today
2 High Street
Kingston-Upon-Thames,
Surrey KT1 1EY

C

GOT something to say? Then get it off your chest by writing to MATCH mailbag — the best read letters page in football.
Address your letters to Nick Wood, "MATCH Mailbag', MATCH, Bretton Court, Bretton, Peterborough PE3 8DZ.

A

Pedal Points,
"Mountain Biker",
PO Box 381,
Millharbour,
London, E14 9TW

PUNCTUATION

Speech marks

In a comic, what people say is put in a speech bubble.

In a sentence, what people say is put into speech marks.
They look a little like the sides of the speech bubble.

"I have finished my homework," Stella said.

start of speech marks   *close of speech marks*

ACTIVITY 1: on your own

Read the words in each speech bubble, **A–F**.
Read the name of the person saying the words.
Write down the sentences **1–6** on page 49, putting the right words inside the speech marks.
Remember: 1 "How much will it cost?" asked Scott.

capital letters

Sentences
1 " _____ ?" asked Scott.
2 " _____ ?" Sam begged.
3 " _____ ," Mr Smith shouted.
4 " _____ ," Nafisa said.
5 " _____ ," Curtis snapped.
6 " _____ ," Emma whispered.

ACTIVITY 2: on your own

Read the words in the speech bubbles **A–F** below.
Read the name of the person saying the words.
Write your own sentences for each of the speech bubbles.

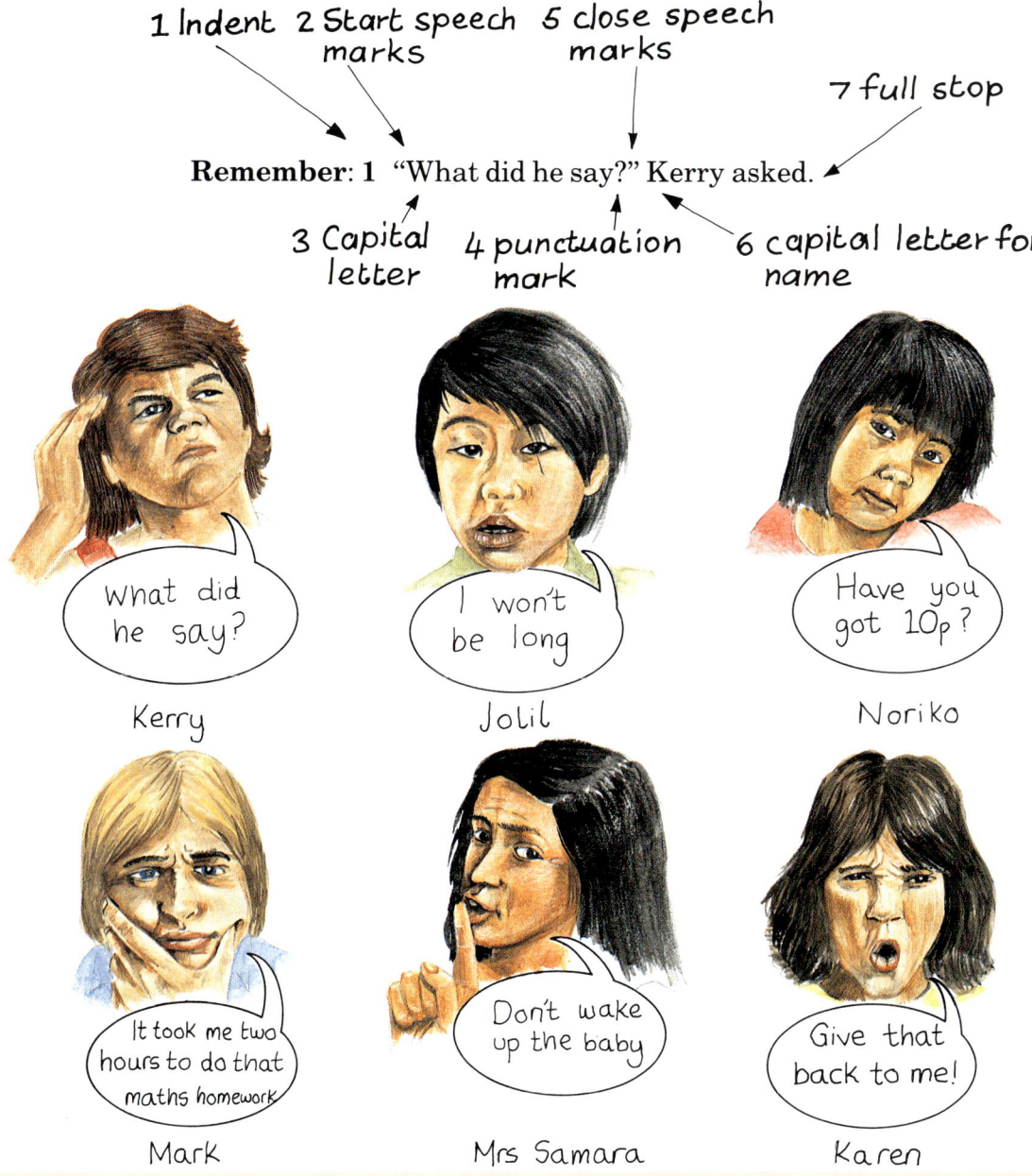

Remember: 1 "What did he say?" Kerry asked.
1 Indent   2 Start speech marks   5 close speech marks   7 full stop
3 Capital letter   4 punctuation mark   6 capital letter for name

Kerry — "What did he say?"
Jolil — "I won't be long"
Noriko — "Have you got 10p?"
Mark — "It took me two hours to do that maths homework"
Mrs Samara — "Don't wake up the baby"
Karen — "Give that back to me!"

PUNCTUATION

ACTIVITY 3: with a partner or in a small group

Work out what words could go in the speech bubbles **A–F** below.

ACTIVITY 4: on your own

Draw six quite large speech bubbles in your book.
Fill each of your bubbles with words that could go in the speech bubbles **A–F** above.
Make up names for the people in **A–F**.
Then write sentences for each of the speech bubbles.
Remember: the points on page 49 in Activity 2.

ACTIVITY 5: with a partner or in a small group

Work out what words could go in each of the speech bubbles in **A–D** below.
Make up names for each of the people in **A–D**.

ACTIVITY 6: on your own

Draw four pairs of large speech bubbles.
Fill each of your speech bubbles with words that could go in the speech bubbles
A–D above.
Write two sentences for each pair of speech bubbles.
Remember: start a new line for each person talking.

"What is the time?" John asked.
"Four o'clock," Dad said.   *new line*

"I don't feel like going to school today," Shefki moaned.
"Go back to bed then dear," Mum said.

Look back at the other points on page 49, Activity 2.

ACTIVITY 7: on your own

Write a small conversation for three of the topics below.

- Buying something
- Playing a game
- Planning a party
- A quarrel
- Trying to find something that you have lost

Paragraphs

A paragraph is a sentence or number of sentences about one idea.
There is usually one sentence in a paragraph that tells you what the paragraph is about.

ACTIVITY 1: with a partner

Put the paragraphs below in order.
For each paragraph write down the sentence that tells you what the paragraph is about.

WEATHER TRAPS

1 Make your trap on a dry day. Put the jar up to its neck in the soil. Put a tiny bit of meat, fish or cheese in the bottom of the jar. This will attract the insects. Balance a block of wood on four stones on top of the jar. This will stop rain from getting into your trap and drowning the insects.

4 Why not make a wet weather trap in the corner of a garden bed. Animals and insects who enjoy the wet weather are often very different from insects you see in dry weather. Looking at what you can find in your trap can give hours of interest.

2 When the rain stops, check your trap and see what you have in the jar. Wet weather is likely to bring out snails or slugs. Do the same thing on a dry day and see what you catch. Always remember to let the insects go when you have studied them.

3 You will need: a glass jar, a piece of meat, fish or cheese: a wood block that will cover the top of the jar and four stones

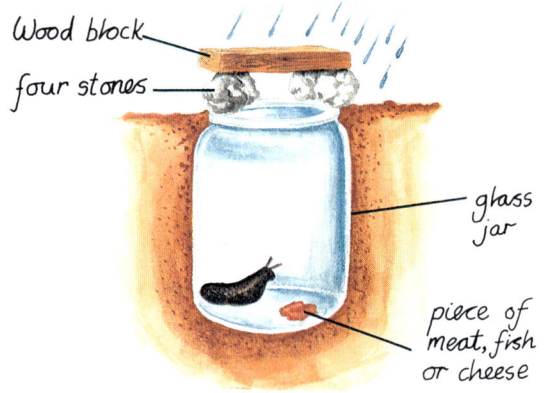

ACTIVITY 2: on your own

Write four paragraphs about the picture below.
Look at the picture below carefully to see how the object is made.
Start each of your paragraphs with the first two or three words from the paragraphs above.
Remember: **indent** a new paragraph.

1 Spelling

ACTIVITY 1: on your own or with a partner

Write down the first letter of the objects below, e.g. **1 = u**

ACTIVITY 2: on your own or with a partner

Write down the last letter of the objects below, e.g. **1 = n**

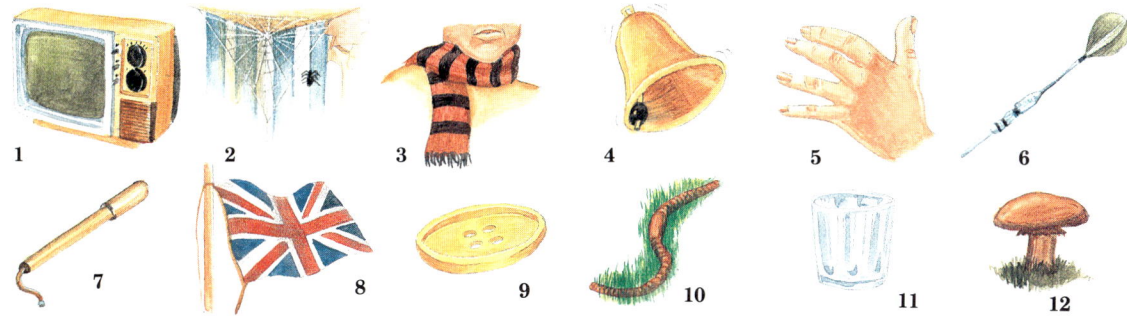

ACTIVITY 3: on your own or with a partner

Write down the middle vowel sound of the pictures below, e.g. **1 = e**
The vowel sounds at the bottom of the page will help you.

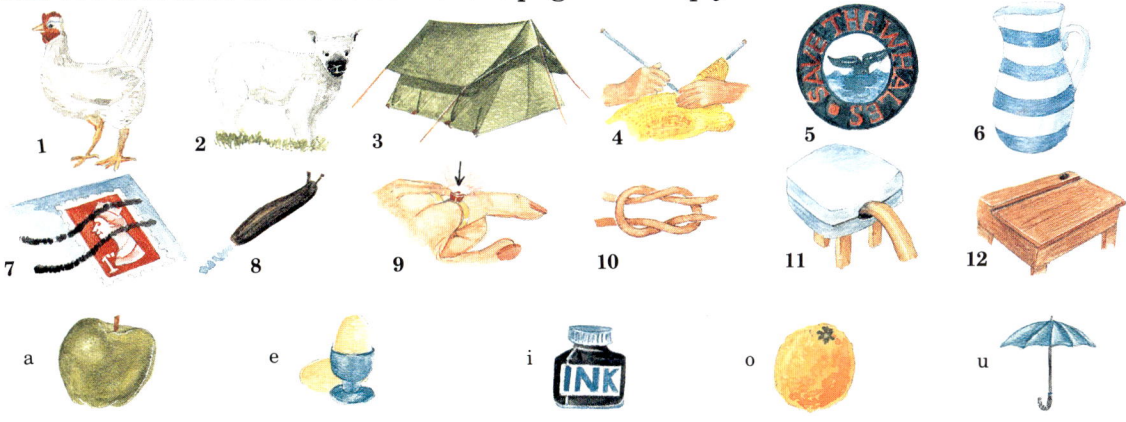

SPELLING

2 Spelling

ACTIVITY 1: on your own

The answers to **1–8** will end in "ad" or "at".
Make two lists of words, one ending in "at" the other "ad".

1 Not thin
2 Another word for unhappy
3 You play cricket with this
4 A pet, with four legs and a tail
5 Another word for father
6 Not good
7 You put this on your head
8 Another word for boy

ACTIVITY 2: on your own

Write down the words you can make using the "it" and "ell" pattern below.
Put two words from each of the lists into sentences.

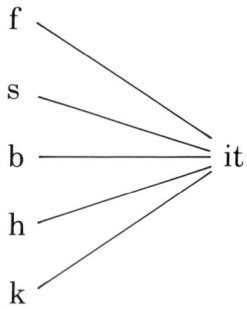

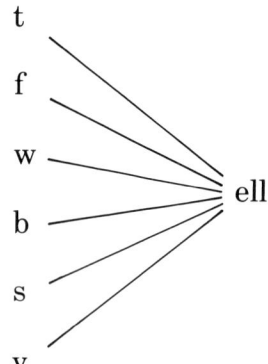

ACTIVITY 3: on your own

With square **A** make a list of words ending in the "et" pattern.
With square **B** make a list of words ending in the "ot" pattern.
Put two of the words from each of your lists into a sentence.

A

b	l	n
g	e	t
j	m	s

B

g	c	l
h	o	t
n	j	p

3 Spelling

ACTIVITY 1: on your own

Write down the words for **1–6** below.

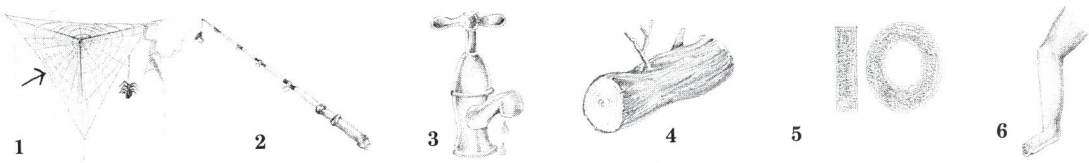

ACTIVITY 2: on your own

Write down the words for **1–5** below.

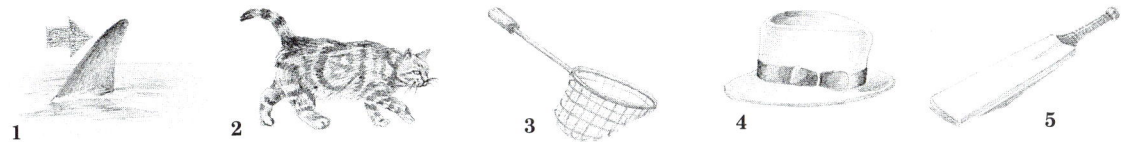

Write down each word again, but **change** the middle letter to "u" each time.
Put three of the new words into sentences.

ACTIVITY 3: on your own

Join the syllables to make words.
Put two of the words into sentences.

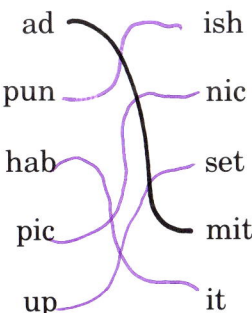

ACTIVITY 4: on your own

Complete the words **A–F**. Use the pictures to help you.

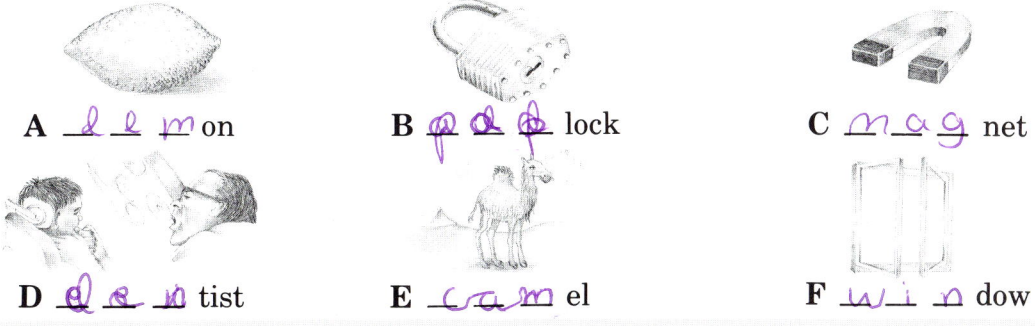

A _l e m_ on   **B** _p a d_ lock   **C** _m a g_ net

D _d e n_ tist   **E** _c a m_ el   **F** _w i n_ dow

SPELLING

4 Spelling

ACTIVITY 1: on your own or with a partner

Write down the **second** letter of the objects below, e.g.

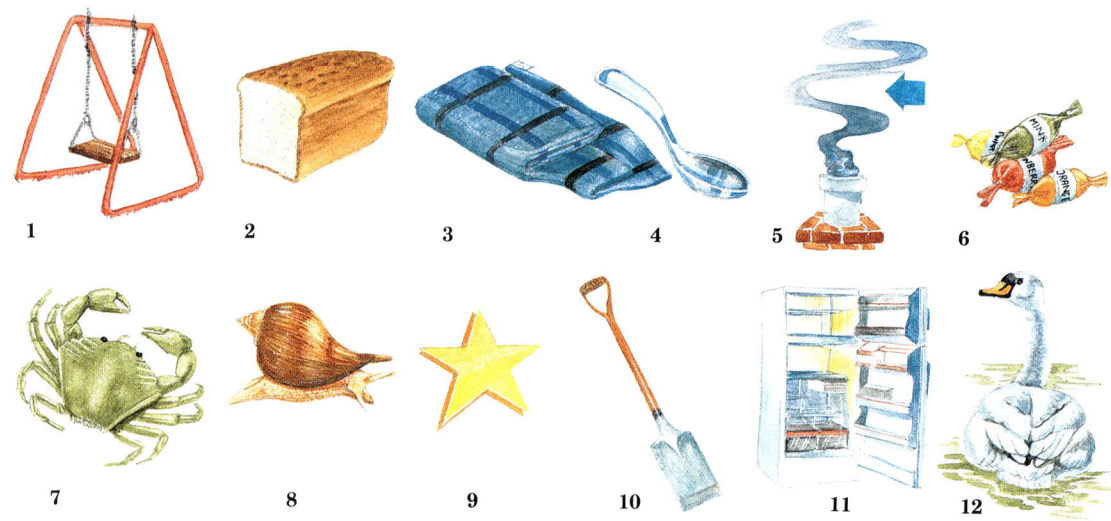

ACTIVITY 2: on your own

Read the words under **A** and **B** below and draw a picture for two of them.
Write down the words in **A** and **B** putting an "s" in front of each word.
Read the new words and write sentences for four of them.

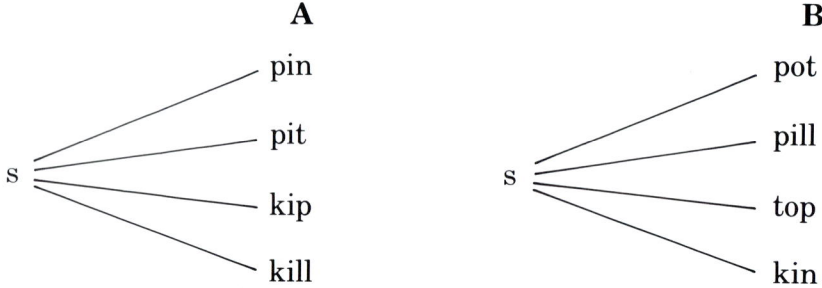

ACTIVITY 3: on your own

Read the words in the box below.
Write down the words you can make using the letters above.
Watch out – you can't always make a word.

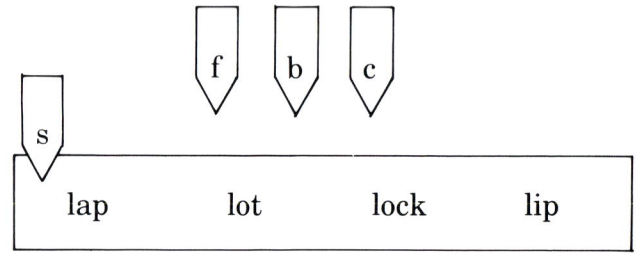

5 Spelling

ACTIVITY 4: on your own

Write down the words you can make, beginning with "ch", "sh" and "th".
Write six sentences, using two words from each group.

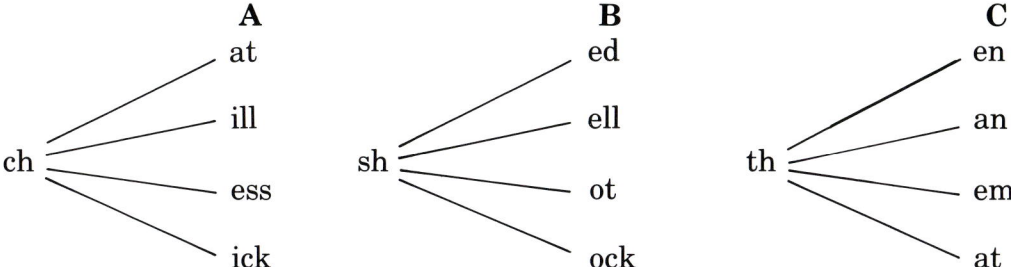

ACTIVITY 5: on your own

Look at the letter patterns in the box below.
Write down the words you can make using the letters above the box.
Draw two pictures for each group.

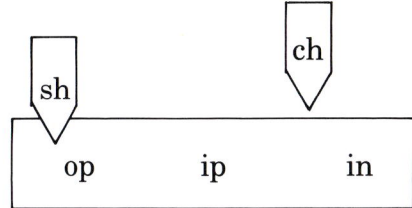

ACTIVITY 6: on your own or with a partner

Write down the first **two** letters of each of the objects below, e.g. *1 = sh*

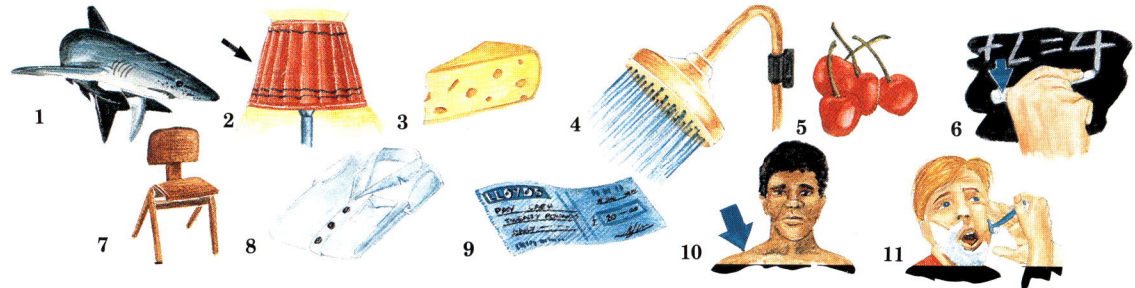

ACTIVITY 7: on your own

Complete the words **A–E**.
Use the pictures to help you.

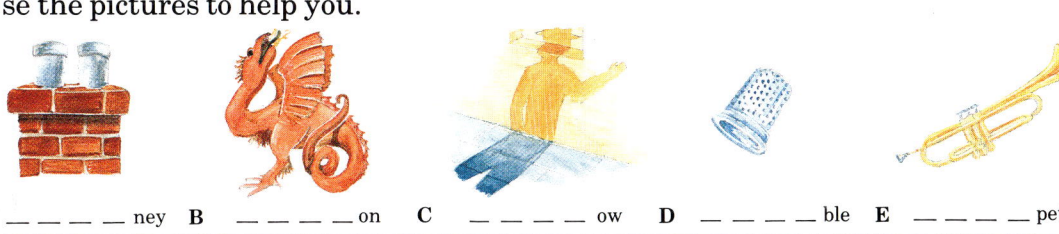

A _ _ _ _ ney   B _ _ _ _ on   C _ _ _ _ ow   D _ _ _ _ ble   E _ _ _ _ pet

6 Spelling

ACTIVITY 1: on your own or with a partner

Write down the letter **before** the last letter, e.g. **1 = s** (wrist)

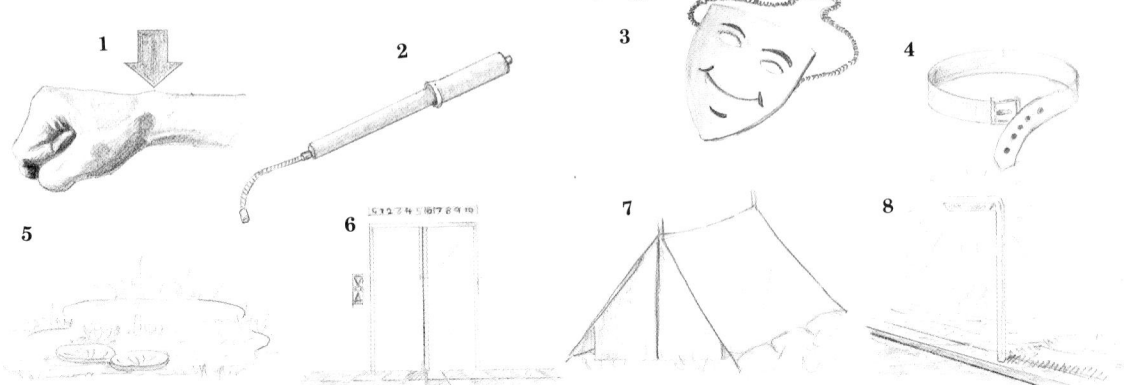

ACTIVITY 2: on your own or with a partner

With square **A** make a list of words ending in "ing".
With square **B** make a list of words ending in "ink".
Put two of the words from each of your lists into a sentence.

A

br	th	s
w	i	sl
st	r	ng

B

w	r	nk
s	i	bl
dr	p	th

ACTIVITY 3: on your own or with a partner

Use the letters in **1–8** to make a list of words ending in "ck", "sh" and "st", e.g.

crack crash

Underline in colour the pairs of words that rhyme.

1 {sma}   2 {ru}   3 {ne}   4 {fi}   {sh}
5 {li}   6 {blo} 7 {cra} 8 {cru}   {ck}
                                          {st}

ACTIVITY 4: on your own

Write down the words you can make, using the "atch" and "unch" pattern.
Make **one** sentence for each pattern, using as many of the words as you can.

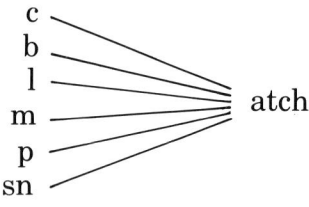
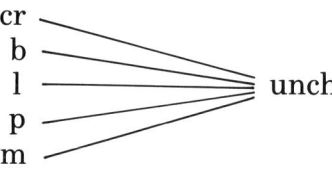

7 Spelling

To make words ending in "x", "s", "sh" or "ch" plural, add "es".

ACTIVITY 1: on your own

Write down the words below, adding "es" to each

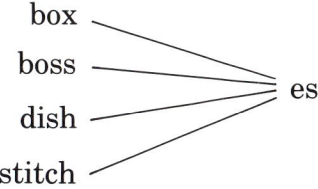

ACTIVITY 2: on your own

Fill each blank in the sentences **1–5** with a word from the box below.
Make sure you **change** the word, to keep the sense of the sentences.

1 "I will have to put some cream on these ___scratch___ ," the nurse said.
2 "If I had three ___wish___ ," Aktar said, "my first wish would be for a thousand pounds."
3 There are no football ___match___ this weekend.
4 Tina watched as Ben opened the card. Now he would see the three ___kiss___ she had put at the bottom.
5 The hunt killed about thirty ___fox___ every year.

> match   fox   scratch   wish   kiss

ACTIVITY 3: on your own

Write down all the words in the picture below which end in "s", "x", "ch" or "sh".
Beside each word, write down the plural, e.g.

1 hutch – hutches

8 Spelling

ACTIVITY 1: on your own or with a partner

Read the words in the boxes below and write them in your book.
How does the "e" at the end of the words change the middle vowel sound?
Tell your teacher.
Fill each gap in the sentences below with one of the words from the boxes.

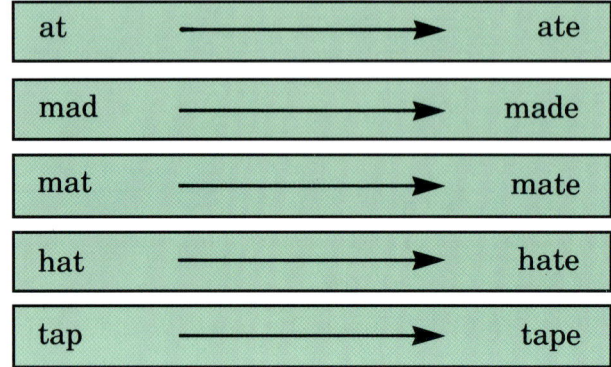

1 "Do you like my new _____ ?" Mrs Hunt asked. "It's for a wedding."
2 "Wipe your feet on the _____ ," Mr Parks snapped.
3 "I _____ having my hair cut," Martin groaned.
4 "You are really good _____ art," Sangeeta said.
5 "There's no water coming from the _____ !" Jake yelled.
6 "We _____ cakes at school yesterday."

ACTIVITY 2: on your own

Write down the words you can make, using the "ake" pattern.
Write a sentence for each list, using as many of the words as you can.

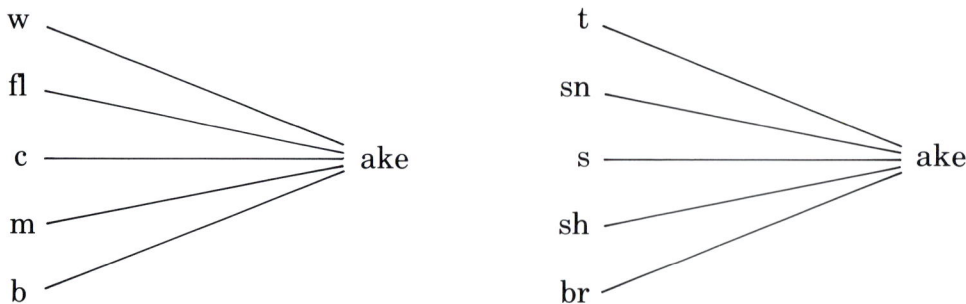

ACTIVITY 3: on your own

Write down the words below and draw a picture for two of them.
Now write down each of the words, taking off the "e" each time.
Draw a picture for three of the new words.

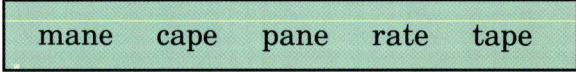

9 Spelling

ACTIVITY 4: on your own

Write down the words in list **A**.
Make a new list, list **B**, by adding "e" to each of the words.
Write down the words for **1–5** using words from one of the lists.

list A	list B
bit	bit
fin	fin
win	win
slid	slid
strip	strip

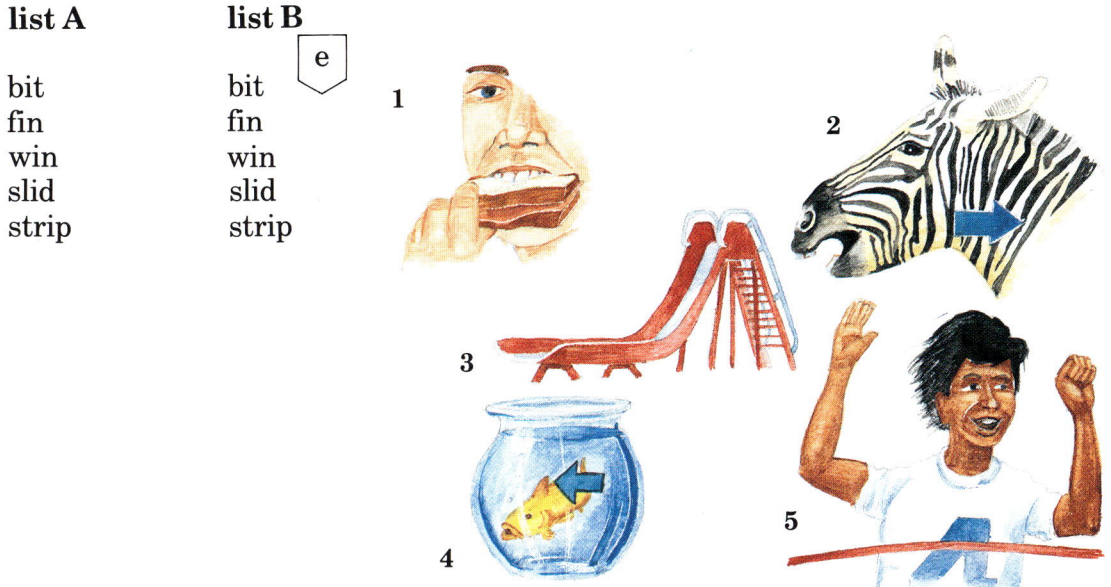

ACTIVITY 5: on your own

Write down the words below and write a sentence for two of them.
Now write down each of the words, taking off the "e" each time.
Write a sentence for two of the new words.

> ripe   ride   spine   slime   spite

ACTIVITY 6: on your own

Write down the missing word in each sentence below.
All the words will end in "ile".

1 "You might as well make a cup of tea _____ you're in the kitchen," Mrs Morgan called.
2 "I have a _____ of washing to do," Mr Adams moaned.
3 "There's some _____ paper on my desk." Mrs Verda said.
4 "Have a sweet," she said with a _____ .
5 It is a half- _____ walk to school.

SPELLING

10 Spelling

Rule: when a word has **one** vowel and ends in **one** consonant (except words ending in "w", "x" and "y"), double the final consonant before adding "ing" or "ed", etc.

e.g. hop – hopping – hopped   strip – stripping – stripped
     one   one   double the   one   one   double the
     vowel consonant consonant   vowel consonant consonant

ACTIVITY 1: on your own or with a partner

Write the rule above in your books.
Write sentences about the pictures below.
Use the words underneath the pictures, but add an "ing" or "ed", e.g.

1 *The key fitted the door*

| 1 fit | 2 plan | 3 scrub |
| 4 wag | 5 fill | 6 grab |

ACTIVITY 2: on your own or with a partner

Write down the words below in your book.
Only add "ing" to words where you double the last consonant.
Where you do **not** double show why e.g.

1 *pun**ch** ✗*   2 *hope*   3 *jog – jogging*
  three consonants   *ends in a vowel*

| 1 punch | 2 hope | 3 jog | 4 look | 5 turn | 6 box |
| 7 chop | 8 shift | 9 play | 10 pat | 11 grin | 12 love |

11 Spelling

Rule: when a word ends in "e" take off the "e" before adding "ing" or "ed".

e.g. hope – hop<s>e</s> – hoping   grumble – grumbl<s>e</s> grumbled

ACTIVITY 3: on your own or with a partner

Write the rule above in your books.
Write a sentence for each of the pictures below.
Use the word underneath the pictures, but add an "ing" or "ed", e.g.

1 *The boys hoped they would be picked for the football team*

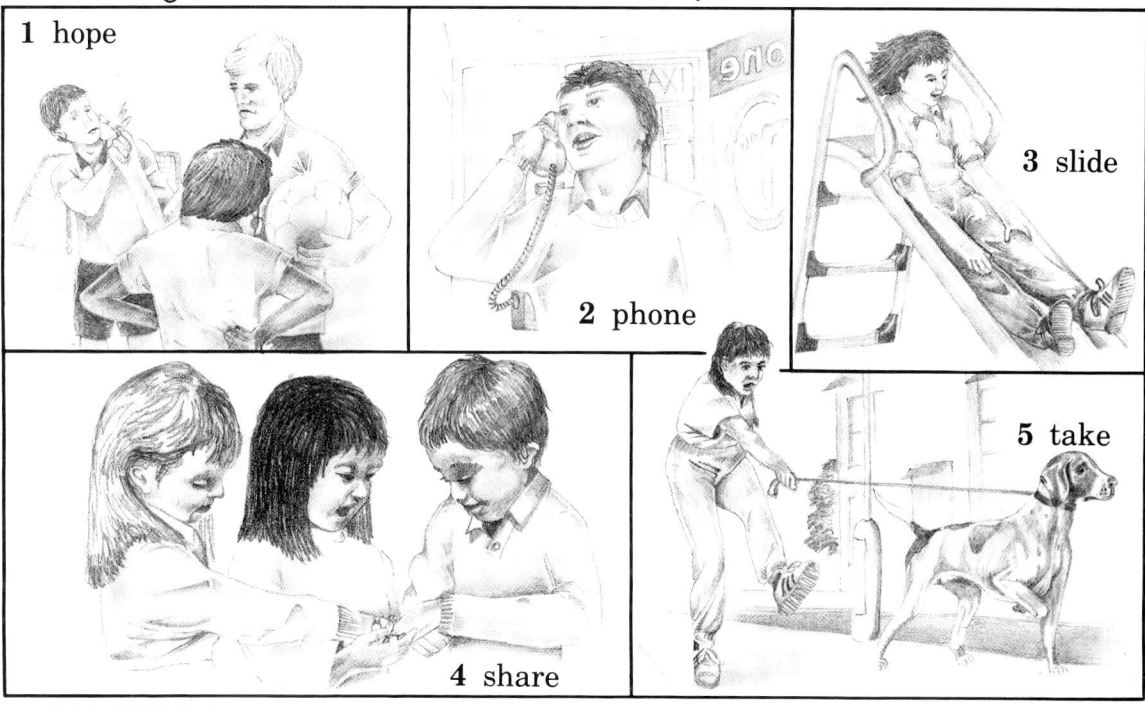

1 hope
2 phone
3 slide
4 share
5 take

ACTIVITY 4: on your own

Fill each gap with one of the words from the box below.
You will need to add "ing" or "ed" to the words in the box.

1 "How many times do I have to tell you?" she _shouted_
2 She _____ it wasn't so late.
3 Azher _____ digging and watched the robin.
4 We were _____ so much noise, we did not hear the door bell.
5 The cat _____ and yawned.
6 The child _____ up and down, holding his foot.
7 As the car _____ down, I saw that Madonna was in the back.
8 "Hit him on the back quickly, "Mrs Lim said. "He's _____ ."

| make | stop | hop | stretch | slow | choke | wish | shout |